TRADE MYTHS

How American Multinationals Create
America's Trade Deficit

By: Enzio von Pfeil

Why trade deficits don't threaten jobs – but
how politicians do

Gotham Books

30 N Gould St.
Ste. 20820, Sheridan, WY 82801
https://gothambooksinc.com/

Phone: 1 (307) 464-7800

© 2023 *Enzio von Pfeil*. All rights reserved.
First published in 2007; re-published 2009 & now, ie in 2023

No part of this book may be reproduced, stored in a retrieval system, or transmitted by any means without the written permission of the author.

Published by Gotham Books (May 18, 2023)

ISBN: 979-8-88775-276-1 (P)
ISBN: 979-8-88775-277-8 (E)

Because of the dynamic nature of the Internet, any web addresses or links contained in this book may have changed since publication and may no longer be valid.

The views expressed in this work are solely those of the author and do not necessarily reflect the views of the publisher, and the publisher hereby disclaims any responsibility for them.

Table of Contents

Chapter I 1
   Trade myth one: imports kill jobs 1
Chapter II 5
   Trade myth two: exchange rates drive trade 5
Chapter III 9
   Trade myth three: trade balance is a national matter 9
Chapter IV 31
   Trade myth four: America's trade deficit is "bad" 31
Chapter V 41
   Trade myth five: foreigners finance America 41
Chapter VI 49
   So what does drive trade flows? 49
Chapter VII 65
   Why doesn't Congress just ban the U.S. multinationals 65
Chapter VIII 95
   Ignore MNCs at your policy peril 95
Graphs, Facts and Challenges 101
Acknowledgements 121
Bibliography 125

*Enzio von **Pfeil** has hit the nail on the head. The pursuit of national economic self-sufficiency, for all its patriotic undertones, is a sorry road to ruin. No single initiative did more harm to the US economy in the Great Depression than the raising of import tariffs through the **Smoot-Hawley** Act of June 1930.*

Sir Ronald Grierson, former Chairman of GEC

Enzio has opened our eyes to the added value of MNCs. There is much truth in what he has to say, but sometimes the truth is hard to swallow.

Alan G. Hassenfeld, Chairman of the Executive Committee of Hasbro

Enzio's approach to trade balances is an important framework. By viewing trade balances from this global perspective, particularly in this age of looming protectionism, we can avoid the repetition of grave mistakes in policy.

Arthur B. Laffer, Chairman of Laffer Associates and Laffer Investments

An interesting thoughtful treatise on us trade deficit. Read this book to become a more discerning investor.

Roland MS Lee, Chartered Financial

*Next to ensuring continued prosperity at home, America's companies that
operate worldwide also create prosperity and thus peace in their host
countries - something vital in this age of increased political and economic
turbulence. I strongly recommend reading this fascinating analysis which is central to understanding a critical factor in the success of those companies.*

Bill Owens, Chairman, AEA Investors (Asia) Limited

Enzio's enlightened analysis could not be more timely, in ingeniously debunking the dangers of traditional mercantilism, namely protectionism. He has convincingly argued the case for a new order of globalization based on an open global financial architecture for the flow of funds and free trade as opposed to the current vested nationalistic monetary priorities. His thesis is a clarion call that should be heeded if the world wants to continue to live in peace.

Terence F. Mahony, Chairman Platinum Advisory, Hong Kong

In my opinion "Trade Myths" is a <u>must</u> read for anyone with the slightest interest in trade. This book clearly makes the point that, as far as trade is concerned, we have moved from a planet of nations to a neighborhood of nations. Enzio von Pfeil makes clear that the interconnectivity of nations resulting from globalization should be seen as a positive for the people of the world and politicians everywhere should accept this.

James E. Thompson, Chairman, Crown Worldwide Group

ABOUT THE AUTHOR

Enzio von Pfeil views the world from his Asian perch. He was born in Namibia and was educated in Germany, England, the United States, and back in Germany. Having studied under Friedrich von Hayek, he received his Ph.D. at Freiburg University in Germany's Black Forest, where he was a member of the prestigious German National Merit Foundation, which awards scholarships to the top one-quarter of one percent of all German students. He subsequently became an Assistant Professor there, specializing in international economics.

Thereafter he joined Morgan Guaranty Trust in New York and Frankfurt, focusing on Treasury matters, subsequently joining J Henry Schroder Wagg in London, as a currency specialist, where he was actively involved in a Chatham House study group. At American Express Bank, London, he worked with private banking clients in Istanbul, Turkey.

In 1987 he became the Chief Economist for Smith New Court Far East in London, with whom he moved to Hong Kong in 1989 and where he has lived since, happily married. In 1992, S. G. Warburg Securities Far East asked him to perform a similar role, which he did until the UBS takeover. Having spent some time with Clarion Securities and with ABN AMRO until 2000 as their Chief Economist, he began providing independent, profitable macro investment strategy with his company, Commercial Economics Asia Ltd., which he since has continued.

He is a regular contributor to Hong Kong's radio station's, RTHK's "Money Talk", as well as to the podcast, "Peter Lewis' 'Money Talk'" . He has published *Deutsche Direktinvestitionen in den USA* (Fritz Knapp Verlag, Frankfurt, 1981), *German Direct Investments in the United States* (Jai Press, Greenwich, and London, 1985), and *Effective Control of Currency Risks* (Macmillan, London, 1988). In London, he was involved with the Royal Institute of International Affairs' Chatham House, where he contributed to the influence of multinationals on trade balances. He belongs to the Hong Kong Forum, which is the Hong Kong Chapter of the New York's Council on Foreign Relations, and to Hong Kong's vision 2047.

Enzio now focuses on preserving his clients' capital via his antidote to Private Banking, totally independent and unconflicted Financial Shield Limited©.

Enzio can be contacted at evp@cea.hk.

© 2023 Enzio von Pfeil

Dedicated to my adored wife, Elizabeth

VII

FOREWORD TO THE THIRD EDITION

Welcome to "host country protectionism"

This book originally was written in 2007, but its findings and messages are as relevant as ever. Indeed, myths are timeless: they are popular, unfounded and insidious platitudes which must be dispelled energetically. Especially with increasing US-China populist animosity flaring, it is vital that policy-makers and thought-leaders step back to re-gain perspective and, thus, composure in matters trade politics/animosities. My re-print seeks to facilitate such perspective and composure.

We provide two sets of solutions, in Chapters III and VII, and then warn of the emergence of an insidious, new form of protectionism in Chapter VIII - and wonder why large corporations inadvertently may be helping to finance the very campaigns of those politicians who are hurting their overseas operations?

In order that politicians and all policy-makers to get proper data upon which to base their decisions, we bring trade balance accounting into the 21st century (Chapter III). There we introduce the concept of "global" trade balances – ones which incorporate the very successful overseas operations of United States multinationals (MNCs). When referring to "MNCs" we do not mean just the well-known brand names; we also mean those smaller American firms working in foreign lands, in "host countries".

In Chapter VII, we provide specific policy recommendations designed to move the trade debate away from "foreigners' unfair practices" to fiscal and educational solutions.

Our deep concern is that if the ideas introduced here are not included in trade policy, an ugly form of protectionism will raise its head, "host country" protectionism (Chapter VIII). This occurs when a company's overseas operations are hurt in the foreign market in which they are doing business. Here is a hypothetical example: a local politician or official in such a foreign market is worried about Congressional action in the parent's home country, e.g. moves to "revalue" the RMB. The local official then targets the American MNC operating in his own host country and starts making life difficult for it – until the respective parent country politicians back off, or the MNC has to reduce its operations significantly in the host country.

The only question then is: why are MNCs helping to finance the campaigns of the very American politicians who are threatening their overseas operations?

FOREWORD

Why a clear message has to be delivered?

Despite the huge reception given to Thomas L. Friedman's *The World is Flat*[1] in 2006, our thinking about trade balances and our measurement of trade balances remains over 500 years old: globalization has left trade balances behind. Mercantilism ruled from 1500 to about 1750, yet the framework[2] it generated – "imports are bad, exports are good" – to account for and explain trade balances persists today. In fact, Pacioli (1445-1517), a friend of Leonardo da Vinci, developed the very trade balance accounting and thus framework used *to this day*.

Here are some of the great names of that bygone era:[3]
1500s: Leonardo da Vinci, Nostradamus, Calvin, Shakespeare and Galileo;
1600s: Newton, Bach and Voltaire, and

---

[1] Friedman, Thomas L., *The World is Flat*, Penguin Books, London, 2006, p. x
[2] Lakoff, George, *Don't Think of an Elephant: Know Your Values and Frame the Debate*, Chelsea Green Publishing, Vermont, 2004, p. 3
[3] Peters, Arno, *Synchronoptische Weltgeschichte:Zeitatlas*, Universum Verlag Muenchen-Solln, 1970, this book consists of panels with no page numbers

1700s: Hume, Smith, Kant, Haydn, Mozart, and Watt.

Who, except for a few scholars, even mentions the names of these Greats today? Curiously, the most popular remnants left are those in literature and music, e.g. Shakespeare's brilliant plays, Bach's, Mozart's and Haydn's wonderful music, and very occasionally, Kant's categorical imperative. But who in this day and age uses only the theories/inventions of da Vinci, Galileo, Newton, or Watt – thereby rejecting subsequent improvements to their important foundations? The mercantilist approach, on the other hand, remains ossified in today's thinking on trade, trade flows and thus trade policy, barely changing over the past 500 years. As Dr. Alan Greenspan notes in his 2007 memoirs, "Current account balances refer only to transactions that cross *sovereign* borders. Our tabulations are loosely rooted in the obsession of the mercantilists of the early eighteenth century to achieve a surplus in their balance of payments that brought gold, then the measure of wealth of a nation, into the country."[4] Mercantilism is an iron cage enclosing protectionism.

---

[4] Greenspan, Alan, *The Age of Turbulence: Adventures in a New World*, The Penguin Press, New York, 2007, p. 354

The result is that this outdated and thus erroneous framework threatens the global operations of US multinational corporations (US MNCs), and thus, the
23 million jobs they create in America,
$341 billion worth of investments in America, and 25%, or $3 trillion, of America's Gross Domestic Product they create.

The perpetuation of the mercantilist mindset means that trade fights have to heat up on Capitol Hill around election time — as regularly as night follows day.

A great deal of that fight is based on the ignorance, deliberately or unintentionally displayed, by many vote-hungry politicians. This is dangerous because if the ignorance gets carried away, the resulting protectionist wave will be felt in hostile international relations, possibly culminating in war (again). It was precisely this die-hard protectionist emotion that radicalized the non-democratic capitalist powers, Japan and Germany, in the 1930s, and today, these are paralleled by the "authoritarian capitalist states" of China and Russia.[5]

---

[5] Gat, Azar, *The Return of Authoritarian Great Powers*, Foreign Affairs, New York, July/August 2007, p. 59 and 68.

Indeed, Russia is of concern, because as Richard Kagan writes: "It is time to stop pretending that Europeans and Americans share a common view of the world...On the all-important question of power...American and European perspectives are diverging...That is why, on major strategic and international economic questions today, Americans are from Mars and Europeans are from Venus: they agree on little and understand one another less and less."[6]

Protectionist sentiment is rising yet again in America and in Europe, especially among the less well-educated labor force.[7] American and European workers, as well as companies operating abroad, stand to lose, not to gain, from such petty politics. When we refer to individual albeit unspecified "American" politicians, we are also including their equally-blinkered colleagues (whether elected or otherwise) in the other developed world as well as in emerging markets. However, in the interest of saving time, we will not mention this qualification each and every time.

---

[6] Kagan, Robert, *Of Paradise and Power: America and Europe in the New World Order*, Vintage Books, 2004, New York, p. 3

[7] Scheve, Kenneth and Slaughter, Mathew J., *A New Deal for Globalization*, Foreign Affairs, July/August 2007, p. 39

A myth is a "...widely held but false belief". Stemming from the Greek root mythos, a further elaboration is made: "A traditional story, either wholly or partially fictitious, providing an explanation for, or embodying a popular idea concerning some natural or social phenomenon or some religious belief or ritual." Politicians everywhere seek to garner votes by exploiting the large following fictitious yet popular ideas command.[8] Small wonder then that such myths, based on the mindset of the 1500s, are still flourishing.

What this book offers is iconoclastic. It questions relentlessly some US politicians' major myths in order to show how mendaciously dangerous and irrelevant these are in our era of deepening globalization. The myths, each dealt with in a chapter, are:
I. Imports kill jobs (so let's protect ourselves against 'unfair' imports);
II. Exchange rates determine trade balances (so let's make other countries revalue their currencies);
III. A trade surplus is national (so imports hurt us);

---

[8] Spengler, Oswald, *Der Untergang des Abendlandes (The Decline of the West)*, Verlag C.H. Beck, Muenchen, 1990, p. 1059

IV. A trade deficit is "bad" (which means that we Americans are living beyond our means), and
V. Foreigners finance America's trade deficit (so the 'bad' foreigner has not only made us have a deficit but also holds the Sword of Damocles over us by financing our deficit).

Chapter VI is a no-nonsense overview of what actually drives trade. Sketching the ideas of key economists, this chapter's intellectual ammunition exposes the myth that trade flows are driven mainly/solely by the exchange rate - a myth many US politicians are stubbornly clinging to in their quest for votes.

Admittedly, the search for votes by satisfying local constituents is a necessity in democratic politics. As Tip O'Neill, the Democrat Speaker of the House during the Reagan Years (1981-1989) put it: "All politics are local." However, mindsets can change, and politicians as well as unelected officials have a duty in bringing about such a change. Indeed, famous historian Arnold Toynbee notes that "habits, unlike instincts, *can* be changed and, faced with the inescapable choice, humanity will prefer painful changes of habit to self-destruction."[9]

---

[9] Toynbee, Arnold, *Change and Habit: The Challenge of our Time*, Oneworld Publications, Oxford, 1992, foreword to his book

To influence people's thinking, one also needs to invalidate past dogma and myth. Noted philosopher Karl Popper wisely taught us that theories are valid until they have been invalidated.[10] But those disproving myths also have a duty to suggest remedies and solutions to fill the vacuum they create. So, Chapter VII provides the remedies that politicians on Capitol Hill can use to alleviate the problems stemming from myths one to five mentioned above:

- One knee-jerk solution would be for the US Congress just to ban US MNCs from producing and selling abroad: that would create more jobs in America and ensure a huge trade surplus and lots of US jobs at a stroke – which surely is what Congress wants? Of course, other powers are capable of hitting back with similar measures, a tit-for-tat unsuited to the age of prosperity created by globalization. History shows how often host countries have expelled foreign MNCs from their own countries. Certain members of Congress risk irking China sufficiently that she will make life harder for US MNCs in China itself. Were US MNCs to be forced home because of Congressional impatience, then foreign MNCs in China would be delighted, of course, with their sudden increase in market shares. Is this what

---

[10] Popper, Karl, *Logik der Forschung*, 8. Auflage, J.C.B. Mohr (Paul Siebeck), Tuebingen, 1984, p. 198 - 226

Congress really wants? Would these foreign MNCs be serious contributors to these politicians' campaign finance coffers, do you think?

This chapter also reiterates the message that trade balances should not be viewed merely as 'national accounts' of the countries concerned. MNCs exert an enormous influence on America's trade balances. In this vein, it is instructive to look at a unique concept called "ownership-based" trade balances, as calculated by the Bureau of Economic Analysis, a prominent research group.

Some practical policy suggestions include: immediate tax relief for workers most affected by globalization; creating apprenticeships and vocational training certificates, akin to America's world-leading professional CFA and CPA programs. Equally important are the educational concepts needed to bolster America's pre-university education, from elementary through to high school.

This monograph has taken years of thinking to keep it concise. As Johann Wolfgang von Goethe quipped: "I don't have time to write a postcard; let me write a letter, instead."

My aim is not to offer a scholarly discourse, but instead to be crystal clear and iconoclastic. Most readers will grasp the arguments intuitively. These arguments are known but have not been packaged conveniently and succinctly.

Globalization is changing paradigms, so we need vigorously to challenge conventional myths in order to stay with the times and create commercial (as opposed to subsidized) employment, as well as neutralize that politically loaded gun of income distribution, especially in America.

The book's contribution to the trade policy debate is to package these arguments into a short, readable, and portable document, one that can be referred to by those involved in making trade policy in the globalized 21st century.

In order to structure the book lucidly, I reverted to my piano and other musical training in Germany and adopted some of the structures that make Bach's Baroque and Mozart's Classical music so clear. This might sound like today's mercantilists, using structures more than 250 years old, but the great musicians have developed these structures so lucidly that they are applied even in modern jazz. I have used the Baroque musical idea of a "cantus firmus", meaning that the same concepts are woven into the text repeatedly in order to be absorbed by the reader.[11] From Mozart's piano

---

[11] Riemann, Musik Lexikon, *Cantus firmus*, Sachteil, B. Schott's Soehne, Mainz, 1967, p. 145 and DTV *Atlas zur Musik*, Band 1, Deutscher Taschenbuchverlag/Baerenreiter Verlag Muenchen, 1977, p. 238-9, and Kaiser, Joachim,

concertos I have adopted his "parallel structures"[12] so that the reader knows where we are headed when discussing each of these five rudimentary trade myths.

While the immediate aim of the book is to reach decision-makers, particularly in Washington and China, the broader objective is to move the thinking away from geographical (i.e. national or nation-state) trade balances and towards global (i.e. multinational) trade balances. This needs to be done to avert protectionism based on myopic mercantilism. Protectionism defeats everyone and the resulting animosity leads to unemployment, followed by social unrest and even wars. It is always easier to blame the "foreigner" than to work on one's own backyard. Most of all, this book is meant to stir some debate in order to solve the problem of protecting American workers from offshoring and, as Prof. Alan Blinder stated in one of his essays: "My main purpose in this essay is to get as many smart people as possible thinking creatively about the problem."[13]

Erlebte Musik – von Bach bis Strawinsky, Hoffmann und Campe, Hamburg, 1977, p. 21 - 71
[12] Hildesheimer, Wolfgang, *Mozart*, Suhrkamp Verlag, Frankfurt a. M., 1977, p. 20 - 21
[13] Blinder, Alan S., *Fear of Offshoring*, CEPS Working Paper No. 119, December 2005, Princeton University, p. 21

Chapter I

Trade myth one: imports kill jobs

How this myth serves politicians: Understandably, politicians want to attain public office and stay in power as long as they can. For that, they need votes. If unemployment among the constituents rises, the incumbents' votes are threatened. In such a situation, the easy reaction of both politicians and their voters is to blame so-called outside forces for fewer jobs.

Of course, there could be several real reasons for the rise in joblessness. These range from bad education policies that do not create employable (i.e., qualified) workers in sufficient numbers, to burdensome taxation, to lack of policy perseverance and poor corporate strategy. One way to avoid the inconvenient truth and deflect the criticism is to put the blame on "unfair" imports for killing domestic jobs.

What would be the result of carrying the logic of "killer imports" to its absurd conclusion? All imports to the US would have to be banned. This would also affect US MNCs that have proliferated abroad and import their foreign-made products back into the US market.

However, unlikely as such a prospect might be in the real globalized world, let us visualize the effects of a hypothetical ban on imports by the US. For starters, most of those imports would have to be substituted by local production, the cost of which would be much higher. This would raise inflation and in turn, interest rates. Higher interest rates result in reduced investment. The growth of manufacturing slows; fewer new jobs are created and more jobs are lost. A rise in the cost of capital sinks the housing market as well as adversely affecting stocks, bonds, and debt markets, which would be focused on diminishing returns on investment (ROI).

In fact, imports allow US companies to make more of what they are good at, thus creating jobs in America: supply creates demand. That is why, when imports rise, so does employment. We have developed The Economic Clock™ for many of the world's economies. Whenever The Economic Time™[14] is good in America, there is

---

[14] Visit www.EconomicClock.com for how The Economic Clock™ works. The Economic Time™ is told by measuring the supply of money and goods in any economy. If there is an excess supply of money and an excess demand for goods, the Economic Time is great. If, however, there is an excess demand for money and an excess supply of goods, the Economic Time is terrible. Visit our website for a constant update of The Economic Clock™ as well as global

an excess demand for goods. So, of course imports rise, as does the number of jobs. How, then, can some US politicians claim that imports kill jobs when the facts support exactly the opposite view? *See chart 1, page 101*

Another question worth asking is: When America employs fewer people in manufacturing, how can her trade surplus *rise* if *fewer* people are manufacturing goods? The share of America's manufacturing employment in total employment shrank by two-thirds - from 28% in 1960 to 10% in 2006.

As fewer Americans are employed on the manufacturing assembly lines, more goods are imported, and that allows American companies to make more of what they are good at – and in this age, these are services. Over the past several decades, there has been a persistent rise in well-paying service sector jobs for Americans; in the 1960s one in two Americans worked in the service sector; by now two in three hold service jobs. In the corresponding period, the country's net balance in services trade has turned into a surplus of $72 billion.

---

investment strategies derived from telling The Economic Time.

To sum up, the idea that imports kill jobs is fallacious for a number of reasons. *The fact is that* thanks to the growth in the services sector, the US export surplus in services has risen significantly.

Chapter II

Trade myth two: exchange rates drive trade

How this myth serves politicians: A second ploy in deflecting criticism of domestic policy that has fostered unemployment is to blame the exchange rate of a country that is running a large trade surplus with America. The simplistic logic of this complaint is that if only that country's exchange rate were stronger, America would have no deficit.

It is all well to hector other nations to up their exchange rates, but it is not easy to have it implemented, especially if the other country has enough economic and political clout in the world. In turn, leaders of that country as well as some voices in the US would demand that the greenback be devalued even more.

What would happen if the US dollar were to be devalued progressively? Among other things, the US would import higher inflation, interest rates would rise, and the value of US assets held by foreigners would shrink. Foreign central banks and overseas investors would wonder why they were holding depreciating assets in US dollars. All of which would lead to a huge sell-off of US assets, including US stocks and bonds. The decline in investment affects the growth of businesses and costs jobs in America.

Myths and probable scenarios apart, what are the facts about exchange rates and trade surpluses? *In fact*, over the past three decades, Germany and Japan have had rising exchange rates AND rising trade *surpluses*, while Britain and America have had falling exchange rates AND rising trade *deficits.*

From 1971 (when Bretton Woods was replaced by floating currencies) to 2007, the Deutschmark[15] rose 2.5 times in its annual average value against the dollar and Germany's global trade surplus rocketed 25 times, to Euro 162 billion.

Japan reveals a similar story. From 1971 to 2007, the Yen rose 2.6 times against the greenback, and Japan's global trade surplus shot up over seven times, to nearly eleven trillion yen.

How, then, can some US politicians claim that a stronger exchange rate kills exports – when

---

[15] According to CEIC Data, the Fed still calculates a fictitious Deutschmark exchange rate, even though the Euro was phased in as of 1999.

exactly the opposite is true in two of the three members of G-3?

Meanwhile, the story is radically different for the Anglo-Saxon economies.

From 1971 – 2007, the British Pound fell by about 20% against the dollar; however, this masks the fact that it had halved in value by 1985. Yet her trade deficit rocketed 463 times during the same period.

And finally to the core argument of many US politicians seeking election or re-election, namely that others' "undervalued" exchange rates are to blame for America's ballooning trade deficit.

In fact, from 1971 - 2007, the US dollar fell by one-third in terms of its trade-weighted exchange rate with major trading partners, but America's trade deficit ballooned nearly 360 times, to over $800 billion. How, then, can some US politicians still claim that a weaker exchange rate propels exports, thus creating a trade surplus?

To sum up, the myth is that exchange rates or other currencies cause American trade deficits. *The fact is that* exchange rates matter in the aggregate only at the margin: we have just demonstrated that countries do not have trade surpluses or deficits because of the exchange rate. Look at Germany's rising currency and its rising surplus – and at America's falling exchange rate and its rising deficit. Of course, individual companies have headaches hedging against their specific currency risks.[16] What really drives trade is the comparative advantage of an economy, not exchange rates. We discuss what really drives trade in Chapter 6.

---

[16] Pfeil, Enzio von: *Effective Control of Currency Risks: A Practical, Comprehensive Guide*, Macmillan, London, 1988, p. 263 - 269

Chapter III

Trade myth three: trade balance is a national matter

How this myth serves politicians: Armed with the myths that imports kill jobs and that ultimately America's growing deficit is because of "undervalued" foreign currencies, it is then appealing to point to a growing trade deficit as a threat to America. Thus, trade balances are seen only from a national perspective: "Fortress America is under threat", alluding to the fear that foreigners, this time the Chinese, are about to spring an economic 9/11 on America.

How convenient to see only the trade balance from the national lens! But in today's interdependent world *the fact is that* everything else -- pollution, security matters, capital flows, and even accounting standards – is viewed from a *global* perspective. Should this anachronistic, mercantilist mindset continues, and legislation, ostensibly designed to protect or promote local jobs be introduced in the US Congress, the move could end up backfiring. It could incite overseas politicians, with similar mistaken notions, to pass laws to discriminate against US multinationals operating there. In extreme cases, even American imports could be restricted or banned.

If such harsh retaliation against US MNCs abroad and US exports were to occur, the US economy would go into a tailspin. It would lead to a spiral of US inflation, higher interest rates resulting in rising joblessness and social stress; the trade war could even escalate to actual hostilities. Two world wars were started partly because of protectionism based on the same arrogance of ignorance displayed by some US and European politicians today.

Even at the level of tit-for-tat trade retaliation, the damage to American jobs would be very significant because of the dominant role of US MNCs. According to the Bureau of Economic Analysis, in 2005 US multinationals employed 30.5 million people – 21.5 million (70%) in America, and 9.1 million workers in their majority-owned foreign affiliates. Meanwhile, majority-owned US affiliates of foreign MNCs employed 5.1 million workers in America in 2005.[17] And those jobs too would be in jeopardy.

---

[17] Bureau of Economic Analysis, *Summary Estimates for Multinational Companies: Employment, Sales, and Capital Expenditures for 2005*, Washington, D.C., 19th April 2007p. 1

Moreover, in this 21st century, (US) multinationals dominate American sales, employment and trade flows, as we discuss next.

As a first step, according to *BusinessWeek*: "Thanks to increasing globalization, roughly 44% of S&P 500's 2006 revenues came from international sources. This compares with only 32% in 2001. The energy sector has the largest international exposure with 55.9%, followed closely by information technology with 55.2%. Interestingly, the exposure for the influential financial sector is only 30.9%."[18] And the share of global revenues of these mostly-American mega-companies rose by 37% over five years.

Secondly, how much of US employment do multinationals account for? About 27% of all non-government American employees work for MNCs in America. Of these, 19% work for US MNCs in America, and 8% work for foreign MNCs in America.[19] How, then, can some US politicians claim that employment and thus trade balances in the US are of purely national nature?

---

[18] Standard & Poor's Equity Research, in Business Week's The Outlook, *Going Ever More Global*, New York City, 20th July 2007, p. 1
[19] ibid. , Table 1

The Bureau of Economic Analysis survey, quoted in the preceding paragraphs, provided data for *non-bank* MNCs only. However, if we carry out the same exercise using *total* domestic MNC employment in America (i.e. including all of the people employed by MNCs in the banking field) in relation to manufacturing employment in America, the results are startling, to say the least.

Based on this approach, in America herself, foreign MNCs employ the equivalent of 64% of the manufacturing labor force. Meanwhile, also in America herself, US bank plus non-bank MNCs employ the equivalent of 151% of America's manufacturing labor force. Thus, in America itself, both MNC groups – banks as well as non-banks - employ over twice the number of people working in US manufacturing. How, then, can some US politicians claim that employment and thus trade flows are purely a national matter?

Thus, MNCs in America employs more people than the purely American manufacturing industry! If we study just the parent companies of American MNCs (i.e., we exclude all foreign-owned MNCs operating in America), they accounted for 19% of all US non-bank jobs in 2004, or 23 million jobs. US MNC parent companies account for over 40% of all American employment in the following sectors: finance, information, and utilities.[20] *See chart 2, page 102.*

How about the importance of US MNCs to the US economy? According to Mataloni and Yorgason, "In 2004, the value added of US parents accounted for 22.6% of the GDP originating in all private non-bank US businesses."[21] They go on to say that the US non-bank overseas affiliates account for 14.9% of Ireland's, 12.4% of Singapore's, and 9.6% of Canada's GDP.[22] Against this backdrop, how can trade flows belong to America alone, i.e., be "national property"?

But there is another reason to be skeptical of national trade balances.

The 21st-century fact is that America's trade balances are dominated by her very own MNCs - testimonies to their outstanding success. However, this success is deliberately ignored by the very politicians who seek to blame exchange rates for America's trade deficits.

---

[20] Mataloni Jr., Raymond J & Yorgason, Daniel R., *Operations of US Multinational Companies: Preliminary Results from the 2004 Benchmark Survey*, Survey of Current Business, Washington, D.C., November 2006, p. 46
[21] ibid., p. 46
[22] ibid., p. 48

Here is the book's key message: We are about to translate globalization – "...the deepening of specialization and the extension of the division of labor beyond national borders..."[23] – into numbers.
We all know that US MNCs operating abroad conduct export and import trade with America. More importantly, however, they buy, as well as producing and selling in overseas markets. How, then, can some US politicians persist in claiming that trade flows are purely national – or are chained to national, geographical borders?

When researching German direct investments in the US, one of my major findings[24] was that companies went to America primarily to serve the onshore American customer by catering to his/her local needs. None of this has changed. How can any company possibly cater to local needs by *not* producing and selling overseas?

In order to gauge the importance of MNCs to America, let us imagine that the US had *no*

---

[23] Greenspan, Alan, op. cit., p. 364: "Globalization – the deepening of specialization and the extension of the division of labor beyond national borders – is patently a key to understanding much of our economic history."
[24] Pfeil, Enzio von, *German Direct Investments in the United States*, JAI Press, Connecticut, 1985, p. 129 - 134

MNCs.[25] If there were no US MNCs operating abroad, US trade flows would be affected radically in four ways:

MNC parents in America could not export to their foreign affiliates;

MNC parents in America could not import from their foreign affiliates;

Most importantly, what foreign affiliates used to produce and subsequently sell in overseas markets would have to be exported from America.

Inputs that foreign affiliates of US MNCs used to buy overseas in their host countries would have to be produced in America, so the parent MNCs could make these products in America. Broadly speaking, these inputs would boost the value of America's exports tremendously; after all, the parent MNCs have to make the goods out of something, don't they?

---

[25] We have conducted similar exercises for Japan and for China and arrived at exactly the same conclusion: MNCs dominate trade flows. On Japan, see: Pfeil, Enzio von, *Japan: Foreign Producers in Japan and the Trade Balance, 1965-1983*, Asia Watch, Smith New Court Far East Ltd., London, March 1987. This work was featured in two consecutive issues of *The Economist* around this time. On China: *Whose Surplus is it Anyway? Globalization has left trade balances behind*, Singapore Straits Times editorial, 18th November 2006, p. 10

Indeed, once we separate US MNCs' trade flows, America's misleading "headline" deficit gets a radically different meaning – and appearance.

As a first step, we look at how US MNCs affect America's trade flows. In 2004, America exported goods and services worth $808 billion. Of this, US parent MNCs exported goods and services worth $253 billion - or 31% of America's total exports - to their overseas subsidiaries. Meanwhile, in 2004, America imported $1,473 billion worth of goods and services. Of this, US parent MNCs imported $276 billion – or 19% of total imports – from their overseas subsidiaries. Of America's total trade deficit of $666 billion in 2004, MNCs accounted for 3.5%. Put differently, had US parent MNCs *not* traded with their subsidiaries, America's deficit would have shrunk by $23 billion ($276 billion minus $253 billion).

Clearly, stripping out MNC-related, explicit trade flows is not where the action is.

The real action is in what US MNCs are doing so brilliantly abroad: successfully sourcing, producing, and selling - and thus reaping huge profits in the host countries in which they operate.

US MNCs' overseas production and sales are over four times the size of America's exports:[26]

Chart 3 on Page 103 illustrates the strength of the growth of this ratio of foreign affiliates' sales to total exports forms 1998-2005. The US trade deficit is *not* due to "bad" foreigners banning imports from America, although we would agree that all governments – America's included – block selected imports. Nor is it due to American citizens "living beyond their means" (see Chapter 5). America's trade deficit mirrors the success of her very own multinationals at producing and selling goods in their respective host countries. But if they are producing goods tailor-made to the needs of consumers in host countries, why should the parents in America be exporting? This is the essence of our assertion that "globalization has left trade balances behind".

The US MNC overseas affiliates have been outstandingly successful at producing and selling abroad, in their respective host countries. Since 1997, their overseas output has almost equaled America's total exports of goods and services. *See chart 4, page 104.*

---

[26] Another broader and more recent idea was proposed by Dr. Alan Greenspan. See Chapter 4 for more about his "diminishing home bias" theory.

In theory, this overseas production could be replaced by exports, which would double America's overseas exports. But it's not that simple. MNCs go abroad precisely *because* they cannot expand their market share by exports alone. Direct investment is therefore the logical avenue for their continuing growth.

The fact that these very foreign governments are host countries to the incredibly successful operations of US multinationals' foreign affiliates tells us how open these governments are to US businesses.

Finally, it is also worth noting how much the foreign affiliates of US MNCs purchase abroad as inputs when conducting their overseas operations. The staggering statistic is that foreign affiliates of US MNCs buy two and a half times more in their host countries than the value of what America exports by way of goods as well as services. *See chart 5, page 105*.

Were the parent MNCs to shut down their overseas operations and sell straight from the U.S., they would need to produce these inputs domestically, back home in America. This, of course, adds to the ultimate value of what the American parent MNCs would be exporting abroad.

It is interesting to trace what proportion of American foreign affiliates' sales are accounted for by (a) exports from America, (b) by their local production, and (c) by their local purchases. These local purchases account for an average of two-thirds of total sales; however, that dominance has been increasing nearly every year. On average, their domestic production in host countries accounts for a further one-quarter of sales. Meanwhile, imports from America are diminishing in importance. This means that these foreign affiliates are increasingly "going local", by cutting back on their imports from America – opting instead to purchase inputs, as well as sell goods, in their host countries. This gets back to the business logic of direct investment: go where the customer is and move with his/her demand. The increase of foreign affiliate purchases in their host countries is noted in *chart 6, page 106.*

There you have it. When reading about US trade "deficits", ignore the role of MNCs at your policy peril! Once the value of what these foreign affiliates purchase and produce in their respective host countries is added to America's domestic exports, it turns out that this superpower has a gargantuan, global trade surplus – *See chart 7, page 107.*

In 2005, for instance, America's global trade surplus of $ 2.7 trillion dwarfed her headline geographical deficit on goods and services of around $714 billion. This means that America's global trade surplus is nearly five times larger than her headline domestic – or geographical - trade deficit. This headline deficit dates back to Pacioli's 15th-century analytical software. But that horrendously outdated mindset still forms the basis of some politicians' misleading and divisive sophistry about "bad foreigners" who are supposedly the root of America's "bad" trade deficit. In reality, the root cause is the activities of America's highly successful multinationals.

Of course, were these very politicians to have their way in getting "quick" trade surpluses and more US employment, they really should propose that all of their own US MNCs' overseas operations should be shut down forthwith and that all their production and thus jobs be repatriated back to America immediately. As we shall see, however, such a quick fix would, in fact, be a financial "9/11" to America's competitiveness, and therefore to its economy and employment (see Chapter 7).

China is the favorite whipping boy of those politicians who attribute America's trade deficit solely to China's exchange rate and its "unfair" trade practices.[27] So let's scrutinize this emotional and deliberately ignorant view by reapplying the principles discussed above: how strongly foreign MNCs operating in China rule her trade surplus:[28]

Similar to our dissection of America's headline geographical trade deficit, let us first understand the enormous role that foreign MNCs[29] play in China's trade flows. In 2007, over half of China's exports were produced by MNCs operating in China. Also, over half of her imports were accounted for by these MNCs. Thus, just over half of China's headline, or geographical trade surplus ($262 billion), was accounted for by MNCs operating in China. *See chart 8, page 108.*

---

[27] This does not mean that we condone China's unfair trade practices, plagiarism of intellectual property, or indeed its export of dangerous goods (witness more recent reports on poisonous pet food and toothpaste, as well as sub-standard tires). But we seriously dispute that these bad *micro* forces actually create China's *macro* trade surplus *more* than the presence of foreign-funded enterprises operating in China does. In addition: why do certain US politicians single only "bad" China out because of its trade surplus with America; are other countries with trade surpluses with America not equally "bad"?
[28] Pfeil, Enzio von, op. cit., 2006
[29] In Chinese statistics, Multinational Corporations (MNCs) are called "Foreign Funded Enterprises". For the sake of clarity, however, we call these "MNCs". We specifically mean the affiliates of MNCs operating in China, but are shortening this to "MNCs" for brevity.

Put differently, once the MNCs' surplus is removed, China's headline, or geographical trade "surplus" is halved. The composition of China's headline trade surplus has evolved as MNCs operating there increasingly dominate her exports. From 1997 – 2007, their share increased by 40%, reaching 57% of all of China's exports in 2007. *See chart 9, page 109.*

This raises the question of how certain U.S. and European politicians can disingenuously claim that it is the "bad" Chinese companies causing China's trade surplus – when it is their very own American and European companies who are embedded in the creation of China's bulging surplus.

Up until now, we have concluded that MNCs operating in China account for over half of her headline trade surplus. But this important conclusion has only been reached by focusing solely on the export and import activities of MNCs operating within China.

The story of China's surplus becomes more revealing when we compare the domestic sales of MNCs in China with their imports for 2007. These startling results show that from 1998 to

2007, the ratio of MNCs' domestic sales[30] to their imports (for further processing on the mainland) rose by one-fifth, leaping from 140% to 170%. This means that MNCs operating in China increasingly opt to produce and sell locally, as opposed to importing semi-finished goods for completion and sales in China. This point is crucial: if MNCs are selling tailor-made goods on the local China market, then this removes the need for China to import them from abroad. Or, for that matter, from the overseas parents of these MNC affiliates. *See chart 10, page 110.*

Let us now apply this same line of reasoning to *all* of China's imports, not just the imports of China-based MNCs. Using this approach, the ratio of MNCs' domestic sales in relation to China's total imports shot up by about one-third over the past decade, to 100% in 2007. This shows that imports themselves no longer meet the needs of the increasingly sophisticated Chinese consumer. Local tastes and whims require locally produced goods. Had European and American politicians banned the MNCs from operating in the local China market, China's total imports would have had to double to meet the needs of her demanding consumers. *See chart 11, page 111.*

---

[30] These exclude what finished goods the MNCs parents export to and then immediately sell in China.

In the light of this, European and American politicians need to sit down and think whether they really want their benefactors and supporters of campaign finances, namely the parents of these multinationals operating in China, to replace local production with imports from the home countries? It doesn't take a rocket scientist to see that the non-European and non-US MNCs would rub their hands together in glee at being given the chance to jump in instead and dramatically increase their China business.

Let us now do a similar exercise comparing what MNCs *produce* in China versus all of China's imports. Were their local production banned by European and US politicians, their domestic production would have to be sourced in the respective countries of the MNCs' parents. In other words, such inputs would increase China's imports significantly:

Analogous to the issue of what MNCs are selling in China, let us first compare the MNCs' domestic *production*[31], with their own imports. The results

---

[31] Again, this refers to their onshore production and thus excludes MNCs' imports of finished goods for immediate on-sale into China.

are even more dramatic than when comparing their local sales to their imports. From 1998 – 2007, the ratio of MNCs' local production to their own total imports shot up about fourfold, from 104% to 153%. This means that MNCs increasingly are opting to make in China what they used to import from abroad. This point, too, is crucial: if MNCs were banned from tailor-making their output according to local tastes, then a great deal of that input would have to come from the host country herself. But the parent MNC would lose out to the other MNCs allowed to continue producing in China. By exporting to instead of producing in the host country, it would be less capable of tailoring the product to domestic needs and regulations and would have to spend substantially more on transporting these goods to the erstwhile host country's market. *See chart 12, page 112.*

Finally, let us compare the MNCs' production in China itself to *all* of her imports. This ratio jumped by nearly two-thirds over the past decade, reaching 90% in 2007. This suggests just how dependent MNCs have become on producing locally in China herself – in order to cater to domestic tastes. Indeed, if European and U.S.

politicians banned such local production by the MNCs, China's total imports nearly would have doubled by virtue of having to ship these goods in from abroad. *See chart 13, page 113.*

So, why don't those US and European politicians bemoaning China's trade surplus with America and Europe just tell their own MNCs operating in China to shut down? These politicians should also then force these American and European MNCs to bring all of their China production, as well as purchases of inputs, back to the US or Europe, so that Americans and Europeans replace their domestic purchases and sales in China with more domestic exports. One does not need a Ph.D. in business to figure out the mortal blow that such legislation would inflict upon these victimized MNCs – not to mention the glee of other countries' MNCs not subject to such short-sighted legislation. We also wonder whether these victimized MNCs would be so thrilled about continuing their financial donations to such charlatan politicians. In closing, what happens if *all* MNC activities are removed from China's trade flows?

Initially, in discussing China's surplus, we removed what the MNCs export from and import to China from her overall exports and imports. The result is that China's headline trade surplus is halved. *See chart 8, page 108.*

With no MNCs in China, there can be no local production or sales there. The result is that instead, China now needs to import these goods from abroad. So, when one subtracts MNCs' domestic activities in China, she would have had a global trade deficit of $1.7 trillion in 2007. In absolute terms, this is over seven times the size of her headline geographical surplus of $262 billion that year. *See chart 14, page 114.*

So, instead of badgering China for its "homemade" geographical trade surplus with America, for instance, why don't these American politicians blame their own MNCs for producing and selling in China - thereby – replacing all US exports of these very goods to China? Or, perhaps the US MNCs operating so successfully abroad should be asked by these very politicians why US MNCs have removed parts of their operations from America and transplanted them abroad. Surely some of the laws passed by these very politicians dealing with taxation and regulatory matters – not to mention other government impositions on MNCs in America, including wage, health care, and negligent education policies – must share the blame for the exodus of US MNCs from America? Similar arguments apply to European politicians garnering votes cheaply by berating China for her "homemade" surplus.

What MNCs want their politicians to force them to relinquish their domestic operations in host countries, opening the door to their German and British rivals? The German and British MNCs would be delighted if Capitol Hill removed a key competitor. Besides, as illustrated by Gladwin and Walter, due to Congressional witch hunts, now only the British and German MNCs get to export cheap Chinese-made goods to America. [32] While U.S. politicians could ban their MNCs from producing in China, do they seriously believe that their parent companies could just make and export these very same goods from America? Hardly. Perhaps these politicians first should understand why MNCs go abroad. Finally, should particularly U.S. or European politicians continue berating China, there is very little to hold angered Chinese government officials back from banning their mainland operation - as has happened before in many parts of the world…

To sum up, trade balances are not "national properties." *The fact is that* a significant portion of the global economy is owned internationally. We have illustrated such international ownership in three vital instances: US MNCs' sales,

---

[32] See Gladwin, Thomas N., and Walter, Ingo, *Multinationals Under Fire: Lessons in the Management of Conflict*, John Wiley and Sons, New York, 1980, page 512 for examples citing "household" names.

employment and more starkly, the enormous influence exerted on trade flows by American MNCs operating incredibly successfully in their local overseas markets. Where trade flows, direct investments must follow if a company wants to stay competitive in the global economy. This maintenance of competitiveness is what keeps creating jobs in any economy. By using this approach, America's headline geographical trade deficit of $714 billion in 2005 explodes nearly five-fold into a global surplus of $2.7 trillion. Meanwhile, in 2007, China's headline geographical surplus of $262 billion implodes over seven-fold to a global deficit of $1.7 trillion. Globalization truly has left "headline" trade balances behind.

Chapter IV

Trade myth four: America's trade deficit is "bad"

How this myth serves politicians: Because trade balances are viewed as national property, many US politicians invariably label the country's trade deficit as "bad". By this reckoning, anyone with a deficit is "living beyond his or its means". This is anachronistic. It is tantamount to saying that people who borrow are bad. Go and tell that to the 8.4 million Americans employed in the financial services industry and earning a total of $250 billion in 2007![33] On this, Dr. Alan Greenspan notes in his recent memoirs that "Such fears ignore a fundamental fact of life: in a market economy, rising debt goes hand in hand with progress."[34] Show us one large firm that is so virtuous (or stupid) that it never borrows! The whole argument is derived from Mercantilist thought of the 18th Century when companies operated mainly within their own national borders and to have huge gold reserves was good – very much in order to finance wars with Medievalism

---

[33] Council of Economic Advisers, *Economic Report of the President 2007*, Table B-46, p. 281-282
[34] Greenspan, Alan, op. cit., p. 346

morphing into the emergence of individual nation-states.

The intellectual backup to this anachronistic sophistry is called the "savings-investment balance". This concept must be challenged vigorously because it is the emotional heart of the mercantilist *mantra*: "Our trade deficit is bad because we live beyond our means." Even an eminent Harvard Professor, Martin Feldstein, writes for instance:

"The basic national income accounting identity tells us that investment minus saving equals exports minus imports. If saving is low relative to investment (in plant and equipment, inventories, and housing), *we must have a trade deficit to bring in the resources to fill the gap.*"[35]

The italicized part of Prof Feldstein's statement just does not make sense. How can a capitalist economy such as America suddenly decree a trade deficit in order to fund spending? Besides, how can a trade deficit fund spending? As Dr. Alan Greenspan put in his memoirs,

---

[35] Feldstein, Martin, *Why is the Dollar So High?* NBER Working Paper 13114, Cambridge, Mass., May 2007, Italics by the author, page

"Those who make the decision to save, however, are not the same as those who make the decision to invest. In fact, if we were to add up the total dollar amount of planned savings and the amount of planned investments for any particular period, they would almost never be equal."[36]

The savings-investment balance ideology decrees that when there is a current account deficit, there must be a Federal budget deficit. However, Dr. Greenspan points out that the Federal budget showed a surplus from 1998 – 2001 – *yet* the current account deficit rose by 82%![37] Do countries with trade surpluses, therefore, consume less than those with trade deficits? Ask any German or Japanese consumer how she links her spending at the local mall to the local trade surplus – or ask any American what America's trade deficit means to her spending habits. You cannot commonsensically connect consumption and investment *via trade balances*. Put laconically, what does your purchase of your own home have to do with your country's deficit with Uruguay? Such is the perniciousness of viewing things from such a sovereign/national perspective in today's purported "globalized" world. Globalization truly has left trade balances behind.

---

[36] Greenspan, op. cit., p. 348
[37] Greenspan, op. cit., p. 349

Philosopher Popper[38] taught us that a theory is valid until it has been proven to be wrong, and the importance of multinationals to trade balances vindicated this: you cannot build a case about bad deficits without first understanding the composition of America's trade deficit. This approach stems mainly from my musical background, and has served me well as a commercial economist who has to make money for clients: if I did not know where the classical or jazz piece that I was playing was headed harmonically or thematically, I could not convey its structure to the listening audience.

In Chapter 3 we introduced the theory we have been propagating since our happy days at Smith New Court Far East in London in 1987: The bulk of America's trade "deficit" is due to American MNCs operating so successfully abroad!

Curiously, Dr. Greenspan puts forth something similar, albeit broader, in his 2007 memoirs. "The most compelling explanation for the historic rise in the US current account deficit is that it stems from a broad set of forces. This does not have

---

[38] Popper, Karl R., *The Logic of Scientific Discovery*, Harper Torchbooks, New York, 1959, page. Also see Hayek, Friedrich A. von, *Die Verhaengnisvolle Anmassung: Die Irrtuemer des Sozialismus*, Walter Eucken Institut, Freiburg i. Br., JCB More (Paul Siebeck), Tuebingen, Germany, 1996, page

the attraction of a single 'smoking gun' explanation such as our federal budget deficit, but it is more consonant with the reality of international finance. The rise appears to have coincided with a pronounced new phase in globalization."[39]

He goes on to say that "home bias" is a key reason for America's swelling current account deficit:

"Home bias is the parochial tendency of investors to invest their savings in their home country, even though this means passing up more profitable foreign opportunities...A decline in home bias is reflected in savers increasingly reaching across national borders to invest in foreign assets. Such a shift causes a rise in the current account surpluses of some countries and an offsetting rise in the deficits of others."[40] The reduction in the home bias of US MNCs has diminished in direct proportion to the explosion of America's current account deficit, as Dr. Greenspan postulates. US MNCs are now investing 21 times more abroad than in the late 1970s. The outstanding success of their overseas operations has left America's current account deficit swollen 53-fold. *See chart 15, page 115.*

---

[39] Greenspan, op. cit., p. 350
[40] Greenspan, op. cit., p. 350

As discussed in Chapter 3, this swelling of the US current account deficit is largely due to the foreign affiliates of U.S. MNCs producing and purchasing inputs abroad.

However, if politicians who dislike America's trade deficit were to follow their mercantilist instincts they could simply ban all imports – and most importantly – make it illegal for US MNCs to operate abroad. In theory, they then could have had a huge trade surplus to the tune of $2.7 trillion in 2005 – not to mention a surge in domestic US employment. Or would they?

What would happen if U.S. politicians, ostensibly seeking to improve America's domestic trade deficit, were to ban their MNCs from operating abroad. Not only do non-American MNCs leap into the breach, but secondly American competitiveness nosedives. By being forced to relocate production and purchasing home to the U.S., the close proximity to their overseas customer base. Thirdly, U.S. employment would shrink. In 2005, U.S. MNCs employed 21.5 million people in America, which represents 14% of the total labor force that year. Lost jobs would have caused U.S. unemployment figures to rocket to about 30 million people, resulting in a jobless rate of 23% and the MNCs out of business. All because politicians wanted a "good" trade surplus. Their 2005 capital expenditure of

$341 billion and their sales of $7.8 trillion would have been slashed, driving America's competitiveness and unemployment further downwards. Fourthly, all this would mean that America's exports would tank, and with it any work related to trade, from trade finance to transport-related manufacturing and services related to shipping and storage infrastructure. Finally, the share prices of American MNCs and any outstanding debt would be massively downgraded. Can US politicians really want to create such an economic "9/11" in the quest to garner votes for their next election?

Of course, no sane politician anywhere would overtly tell his/her own major corporations to come back home. But, as we discuss more in Chapter 7: perhaps these very US politicians need not even ban their own MNCs' overseas operations explicitly: they just need to anger the host country, such as China to the point where she ejects the American – and other foreign - MNCs herself. Recent events have highlighted the volatility of the situation. These have involved protests over the Olympic flame, and international objections to China's actions in Tibet. These have led to anti-French demonstrations outside Carrefour outlets in China. It's a short step from there to the Chinese authorities deciding that enough is enough and asking them to leave.

At the very least, Beijing could make life less pleasant for US MNCs operating in China – and make life *more* pleasant for *non*-US MNCs operating in China. It is very possible, for instance, that Congressional bickering about low-quality Chinese toy exports in the third quarter of 2007 prompted various Chinese officials to force Mattel to *kow tow* by way of a public apology to China. Equally, with European politicians whining about the "poor quality" of Chinese products one cannot avoid the impression that the European companies producing in – or buying from – China does not have their own adequate quality control systems in place. Is there any law banning such internal quality controls? To say the least, Congressional bickering has not made Mattel's life in China easier.

Either way, these very US politicians ranting about China's "undervalued" currency are going to make life for their own American MNCs operating in China and elsewhere much more difficult, if not impossible. We wonder in such circumstances whether these disaffected MNCs will want to continue voting/ moreover contributing to such politicians' campaign finance coffers? What would motivate American companies to finance certain American politicians whose actions and legislation are threatening not only their management but also their bottom line and thus workforce?

In fact, when we compare America's traditional current account (which spuriously is meant to represent her savings-investment imbalance to America's global trade surplus as introduced in Chapter 3, America has a huge *excess* of savings.

In 2005, America's global trade surplus including the sales of overseas MNCs, stood at $2.7 trillion, equal to about one-fifth of America's GDP. Meanwhile, her headline current account deficit of $755 billion was about one-quarter the size of her global trade surplus. So which number is more reflective of the 21st century's trade realities? *See chart 16, page 116.*

To sum up, when viewed through today's prism of globalization, *the fact is that* America has a huge global trade surplus and thus excess savings – even if, as we discuss next, a great deal of such savings must be stashed abroad by US MNCs because of legitimate tax reasons. Besides, what is so bad about borrowing? Corporations do this all the time. Does this make them bad? If so, how do we label bankers then? Are they "enabling" those "immoral borrowers"?

Chapter V

Trade myth five: foreigners finance America

How this myth serves politicians: Another consequence of trade balances being viewed as national property that is intellectually buttressed by the "savings-investment balance" framework is the widely held belief that the America's fiscal deficit is financed dangerously by foreigners. This creates an emotional mindset of vulnerability – one that makes it easy for politicians to then blame the foreigner for America's ills. In such a siege mentality and a search for invulnerability, congress could decree that foreigners are prohibited from holding any US federal debt. So, all foreigners dump their US federal bonds and drive bond yields through the roof. But how can the U.S. Congressional politicians force Americans to buy up these bonds? Were these bonds not bought by Americans, their prices would plunge with rocketing yields. Vastly higher yields drive up mortgage rates, killing the housing market. Also, other truly dangerous financial innovations like sub-prime debt and collectivized debt obligations come unstuck, as we have seen in 2007 – 2008, sending financial markets into tailspins. With foreigners dumping bonds, the dollar plunges, driving up inflation so the Fed has to tighten. And on goes the imaginary scenario – which morphed into reality with the emergence of the subprime crises in the second quarter of 2007. Are these financial storm clouds of 2007-2008 predictors of what Congressional trade bashing could inflict on global financial markets?

But what is the reality of US savings? *In fact*, Americans themselves, along with many US hedge funds and US multinational corporations' foreign subsidiaries (many of whose financial arms are domiciled in the Caribbean because of high US taxes as well as ridiculously onerous reporting requirements), own huge portions of America's federal government debt – offshore. So, this need not make people scared that America is vulnerable to a sudden, foreign pullout.

Let's now delve into what is meant by "foreign ownership" (just as we have dissected America's trade "deficit"). What does "foreign" actually mean?

Foreign ownership figures misleading. At the end of 2006, the *stock* of US Treasury securities outstanding was US$8.7 trillion.[41] Of this, 52%

---

[41] ibid. , Table B-89, p. 334. There are two sources for the *stock* of foreigners' holdings of US Treasury securities: a) Dept. of the Treasury, Federal Reserve Bank of New York,

was held by the Federal Reserve and Government accounts, while private investors held 48%. There is a sub-category within private investors, "Foreign and International". These foreigners held 25% of all Treasury securities. While this is up from 1995"s 14% share, remember that Americans still own 75% of their own debt. When politicians sound alarms that "...foreign ownership of nearly half of US debt was a source of great vulnerability,' and that 'the economy can be held hostage to the economic decisions being made in Beijing, Shanghai and Tokyo, '"[42] they are referring to only the portion of US Treasury securities that are held overseas. This statement is not only misleading, but it is also perplexing. Why should foreigners, in this age of globalization, *not* own some of the debt issued by the world's most sophisticated Treasury? Besides, what does "foreign" really mean? Are we talking about "pure" foreigners, or also about US citizens as well as MNCs with

---

Board of Governors of the Federal Reserve System: *Report on Foreign Portfolio Holdings of US Securities,* and b) Office of the Management and Budget, *Foreign ownership of US Treasury securities: Analytical Perspectives.* There are two sources for the *flows* of foreigners' purchases and sales of US Treasury securities: a) US Dept. of the Treasury: *Treasury International Capital Data*, and b) The Federal Reserve Board's *Flows of Funds*.
[42] Stanton, Elizabeth, *Foreign US Notes Rise to 80 Percent; Treasuries Irresistible*, Bloomberg.com, 6th June 2007

overseas financial vehicles? My suspicion is that "foreign" refers to anyone whose firm is located outside of the US; however, the nationality that actually *owns* that overseas money is irrelevant.

More foreign private ownership of US debt. What is happening is that foreign *private* holdings are increasing while foreign *official institutions'* holdings are decreasing. In 1978,[43] foreign official institutions held 86% of long-term US Treasury debt held by foreigners, with the remaining 14% held by foreign private institutions. By June 2006, this had changed radically: the share of foreign official institutions fell to 70%, while that of foreign *private* institutions more than doubled, to 30%![44] One safe conclusion is that private individuals, including US multinationals, have increased their share of what "foreigners" own of US debt.

US MNCs' ownership of federal debt. Even if there appears to be no data available on how much US Treasury debt is held by US MNCs, a firm and historical linkage must exist. After all, what do U.S. MNCs do with at least a portion of all of that money they are making in their fabulously successful overseas operations?

---

[43] Dept. of the Treasury, Federal Reserve Bank of New York, Board of Governors of the Federal Reserve System, *Report on Foreign Portfolio Holdings of US Securities, June 30, 2006*, May 2007, Table 6, p. 10
[44] ibid. , Table 6, p. 11

Optically, there is an extremely good "fit" between the overseas investments of U.S. MNCs and "foreign" ownership of America's federal debt. This suggests that plenty of U.S. government debt is held legally by American MNCs in legitimate foreign tax havens. *See chart 17, page 117.*

Importantly, the good news, with the official share receding, is that foreign governments cannot punish the US as harshly as before by withdrawing their holdings; these have shrunk, thereby reducing America's vulnerability. Besides, with the foreign private portion of such ownership increasing, the impact of governments dumping their holdings of US debt is diminished.

Limited non-American options. The other point with which to counter the "foreign pullout" threat is to ask where will private, institutional and official foreign investors go? There are no other capital markets anywhere offering even remotely the depth, liquidity, or indeed, sophistication of America's capital markets.

Unsurprisingly, America dominates global domestic bond markets.[45] Indeed, according to the Bank for International Settlements, America's domestic bond markets – i.e. excluding her gargantuan issuance of Eurodollar bonds – are larger than the *combined* value of Europe, Japan, the United Kingdom plus Switzerland. *See chart 18, page 118.*

---

[45] Bank for International Settlements, *Quarterly Review*, December 2007, Table 13B, can CEIC Data Ltd. The data for China are for the markets that international investors can participate in: the red chips and H-shares.

This makes one wonder how certain U.S. politicians can argue "choice": as if investors can choose where to invest the money that they have gleaned from selling "all" dollar bonds. Surely if they enter the smaller markets, they – logically – would drive the price of non-dollar bonds up so much that they would become unattractive.

This also applies to America's stock markets, whose market capitalization exceeds the combined value of the stock markets of Continental Europe, Japan, the United Kingdom, China and Switzerland.[46] *See chart 19, page 119*

To sum up, it's a myth that foreigners finance the US fiscal deficit. *The fact is that* America is *not* vulnerable to foreigners suddenly pulling out of US capital markets. First, foreigners own only 25% of the US Federal debt. However, within this category, the holdings of private institutions are rising while those of official ones are falling, meaning that the foreign governments cannot hold American finance hostage. We also sense that a great deal of these foreign private holdings of US Federal debt belong to the offshore companies of US MNCs and American money managers including hedge funds themselves who legitimately are avoiding high US taxes and

---

[46] Economist, The, *Pocket World in Figures*, London, 2007 edition, p. 68

onerous reporting requirements. Finally, what would foreigners do if they pulled out of the US capital markets? The US markets are, in fact, larger than all the other four major capital markets *combined*.

This ends our review of stubbornly-held trade myths based on a framework of thinking about and accounting for trade that is 500 years old and that to this day is being exploited by certain politicians to garner votes cheaply. Globalization truly has left trade balances behind – and policy makers are ignoring MNCs at their peril when studying trade flows and thus trade policy. So how to catch up?

Chapter VI

So what does drive trade flows?

Having challenged these five trade myths, let us now move away from the arrogant simplicity of some US politicians' statements that trade is only about "undervalued" exchange rates and "unfair" trade practices. Was that the case, some of the best economists for over 300 years would *not* have continued studying what actually drives trade flows. Or have these top economics brains just been wasting their – and thus our – time? I think not. I'll side with the humility of the economists and not with the arrogance of ignorance of certain politicians any day.

Before providing his perspicacious overview, Lord Roll wrote the following in his marvelous *A History of Economic Thought*[47]:

"...the ultimate dilemma of the relation between politics and economics, that is, between those who wield power...and those who advise either directly or through the influence of their theoretical work, would still remain to be resolved. Plato, in speaking of philosopher kings,

---

[47] Roll, Eric Lord, *A History of Economic Thought*, Fifth Edition, Faber and Faber, London, 1992, p. 578-9

took one alternative view, Kant was more pessimistic:[48] 'That kings should philosophize or that philosophers should become kings is not to be expected; nor is it to be desired: for the possession of power ineluctably corrupts the free judgment of reason."

We emphasize this because the whole reason for writing this book is to contribute to the policy debate about trade balances by being iconoclastic. We cannot resolve Lord Roll's "ultimate dilemma" either but hope to have illustrated graphically the consequences of adhering to and advocating the five hypocritically dangerous trade myths discussed previously.

Here is a particularly useful summary of why nations trade in the first place, written by Prof. Ingo Walter:

"The reason that nations trade is because it pays to do so. On the supply side, the availabilities and cost of labor, capital, raw materials, and other inputs differ among countries, as do technology and the efficiency with which inputs are used; therefore, the costs of tradable products will differ. On the demand side, tastes and incomes tend to differ among countries. Supply and

---

[48] Kant, Immanuel, *Zum Ewigen Frieden*, Koenigsberg, 1781, p. 48

demand forces produce international price differences, which in turn create the profit opportunities that trigger international trade flows. Sellers can market their goods and services abroad at a higher price than they could obtain at home, and buyers can purchase goods and services from abroad at a lower price than at home. These possibilities make individuals, groups, and countries more productive and better off. They create the gains from international trade." [49]

Ultimately, then, what drives trade is absolute and comparative advantage: countries specialize in producing what they produce best. But before discussing this, it is important to understand the etymology of the concept,[50] – as it bears precisely on why we have been railing against these five trade myths.

People have not always believed in the idea that international trade is a "win-win" proposition, however. Mercantilists viewed the economic system and thus international trade as a "win-

---

[49] Walter, Ingo and Areskoug, Kaj, *International Economics*, Third Edition, John Wiley and Sons, New York, 1981, page
[50] I have relied heavily on the marvels of Wikipedia in creating this intellectual tool of convenience. Many thanks to each of Wikipedia's contributors. Also see: Blinder, op. cit., p. 3-4

lose" proposition, whereby one nation's gain is another's loss. This mercantilist mindset– during which today's trade balance accounting was developed – dominates the American political subconscious through the "American System", which we discuss later in this chapter.

First, how did we get to today's "trade deficits are bad" mercantilist mindset in the first place?

Mercantilism (1500-1750) replaced the agriculturally-oriented medieval worldview, which was imbued with religion and fatalism. While there is no unified "mercantilist school of economic thought" that outlines a "mercantile economy", its etymology derives from the Latin *mercari*, which means "to run a trade", and from *merx*, meaning "commodity". Victor de Riquieti, Marquis de Mirabeau, coined the term "mercantilism" in 1763. Mercantilism flourished because it was a useful ideology with which to promote and justify the emergence of nation-states and thus the financing of huge wars in Europe, not to mention the Continent's imperialism abroad.

The mercantilist mindset of "if I win, you must lose" has to do with the concept of **absolute advantage**: a country has this advantage if it can produce the good much more cheaply than the other country. Remember that mercantilism was pre-industrial, so the bulk of the trade was in agriculture, hence the trade in only one good or at least one category.

This feeling of vulnerability resulted in Mercantilism's key "win-lose" elements, namely:
A nation depends on production and thus on its supply of capital;
Thus, a trade surplus is "good" while a deficit is a threat;
Thus, the government should encourage exports and discourage imports;
This can be achieved if the government plays a protectionist role, and more broadly, through plenty of government intervention, and

Do you see how strongly this mercantilism is mirrored in today's trade myths, particularly myths three to five?
A trade balance is national property;
Thus, a trade surplus is vital, and thus good, and Foreigners finance America.
This is partially because of America's "special relationship" with mercantilism.

We will get back to this when we discuss the "American School" below. Indeed, mercantilism is embedded in the American political subconscious, particularly in the Republican Party as we discuss shortly.

During the 18th century, while Britain was undergoing its first industrial revolution, primarily Scottish thinkers developed the opposite idea - namely that international trade actually is a "win-win" proposition. The fathers of anti-mercantilist thought and thus of our "free markets" thinking are David Hume and Adam Smith. Their work led to David Ricardo's development of "absolute" and "comparative" advantage, antidotes to the mercantilists' "if I win, you lose" mindset. Maybe the seed for this change in thinking was that the dominance of commoditized agriculture was waning, while that of differentiated industrial goods was on the ascendant.

David Hume (Edinburgh, Scotland, 1711-1776) believed that trade stimulates a country's economic growth. He felt that countries could feed off each other's wealth, thereby creating a ***"prosperous community"***. He also disbelieved the mercantilists' goal of a constantly positive balance of trade: the surplus would result in a rising money supply, driving up inflation and thus making the nation with the trade surplus lose out in cost-competitiveness. Hume influenced Adam Smith.

Adam Smith (Kirkcaldy and Edinburgh, Scotland, 1723-1790) is considered the father of classical or *laissez-faire* economics. So, while there never was a mercantilist economy, Smith developed the framework for a "classical economy." In developing this, he replaced the concept of protectionism promoted by the mercantilists. In ***An Inquiry into the Nature and Causes of the Wealth of Nations*** (1776), his two main criticisms of mercantilism were that Protectionist tariffs further a nation's economic interests, and Huge gold reserves are vital for a country's safety and thus economic success. This critique was then used by David Ricardo to develop the theory of comparative advantage.

Below are Smith's other notable ideas that pertain to the trade balance debate:[51]

"The invisible hand" is another concept crucial to our subject of trade myths. It is all right to think of your own self-interest because in so doing you will serve the common good much more effectively than by overtly seeking to serve society. Smith wrote: "It is not from the benevolence of the butcher, the brewer or the baker, that we can expect our dinner, but from their regard to their own interest." (Book 4, Chapter 2). By pursuing "...only his own gain, and he is in this...led by an *invisible hand* to promote an end which has no part of his intention." Specifically, if US MNCs are *not*

---

[51] Smith, Adam, *The Wealth of Nations*, edited by Andrew Skinner, Penguin Books, London, 1976, page

allowed to promote their self-interests by producing abroad, (see next Chapter), the American as well as the global economy, will suffer hugely – and war will result yet again. Is this what some US politicians want in order to rack up large US trade surpluses by forbidding or making it difficult for US MNCs to produce abroad? Why do some US politicians insist on making the lives of their own nation's MNCs – and, as we discuss in Chapter Seven, the lives of their own, American workers - so difficult, we wonder?

The acknowledgement that it is important to pursue one's own self-interest led to another of Smith's insights: in today's jargon we call it **"win-win"**. He writes that "…a voluntary, informed transaction benefits both parties" – contrary to the mercantilists' agriculturally-based "If I win you have to lose" mindset. The reason that both parties win is that the buyer places greater value on what the seller is providing him than the money he is giving the seller: he is about to get a great return on his investment.

Another facet of the invisible hand is that **markets self-correct**, so there is no need for government intervention. In the context of our theme: why not let the MNCs continue doing what they are best at, without politicians telling them how to run their corporations?

A final contribution of Smith is his railing against **vested interests.** He repeatedly attacks groups that seek to use their collective influence to manipulate the government to do their bidding. "People of the same trade seldom meet together, even for merriment and diversion, but the conversation ends in a conspiracy against the public, or in some contrivance to raise prices." (Book 1, Chapter 10). In the context of our theme: are some of these US politicians perhaps protecting the interests of certain constituents (who fund them or vote for them) while feigning concern about America's trade deficit?[52] Put another way, why should US MNCs keep filling the campaign coffers if these very politicians are jeopardizing their overseas businesses *and thus American jobs in America herself?*

David Ricardo (London and Gloucestershire, England, 1772-1823), another classical economist, took his cue from Smith's "win-win" insight and in 1817 developed the concept of "comparative" advantage. Remember that the mercantilist mindset was "I win, you lose", while that of the classical economists was "I win, so you have to win – otherwise, there is no deal." He outlines the concept in his most famous work, *Principles of Political Economy and Taxation*":

---

[52] This is the point emphasized in Spengler's *Decline of the West*, op. cit., p. 977

Comparative advantage exists when one country's production costs are *relatively* lower than another's. A standard example of Ricardo's was that Portugal was a far more efficient producer of wine than England was, but England was a far more efficient producer of cloth than Portugal was. So, if Portugal specialized in wine, and England in cloth, both sides would gain.

Prof. Paul Samuelson offers us a graphic illustration of comparative advantage in his book, *Economics*. In City X, the best lawyer also happens to be the best secretary. But he obviously would earn more money by focusing on being a lawyer, rather than having to apportion part of his day to secretarial duties. Therefore, if he hires a secretary, he makes far more money by paying her and focusing on his more lucrative legal work, than by doing both and thus losing commercial focus.

It is worth pointing out that with the industrial revolution underway, a comparative advantage made sense because countries had more goods than just undifferentiated agricultural commodities to offer one another. **James Watt** was born in Greenlock, Scotland, in 1736, 14 years after Smith. As of about 1760, the industrial revolution began gripping primarily Great Britain. He invented the steam engine that boosted industrial production significantly.

In his *Principles*, Ricardo also emphasizes his opposition to trade protectionism. He felt that British tariffs on the imports of agricultural products, "Corn Laws", would result in British farmland being cultivated less productively than if there were no import tariffs. This ties in with our theme of trade myths: those US politicians calling for protectionism under the guise of stricter quality control of imports, or under the guise of pointing to the empirically shaky concept of "undervalued" currencies, or indeed under the guise of such emotionally explosive terms as "unfair trade practices" must believe that American workers would be more productive behind protectionist walls. So these very politicians obviously disagree with Ricardo. We wonder how they possibly could disagree with this Portuguese-Scotsman's common sense?

Eli Heckscher (Stockholm, Sweden, 1879-1952) and Bertil Ohlin (South of Sweden, 1899-1979) developed the Heckscher-Ohlin (HO) theorem and the general equilibrium mathematical model. HO takes Ricardo's comparative advantage theory one step further by honing in on *factor endowments*. A country has a comparative advantage in producing a certain product if it is relatively well endowed with inputs that are used intensively in producing the product. Their model predicts global trade and production by using factor endowments as inputs. Here, countries will export those goods that use their most abundant factors and will import those goods where their own production factors are scarcest. In Chapter 7 we will tie such factor endowments to improvements in America's pre-university and vocational educational system – and thus to equalizing its increasingly skewed income distribution – which is tinder to the fire of domestic revolution, as history has demonstrated time and time again.

This ends a cursory overview of what some of the world's leading economists think drives trade. As you can see, the basis for trade is cold comparative advantage, not the appealing sophistry of currency or trade manipulation.

Before we continue, we need to re-emphasize that in the course of researching our subject, we stumbled across the intriguing idea that while Britain totally accepted Adam Smith's repudiation of mercantilism and accepted classical free-market economics, America rejected classical economics and instead preferred neo-mercantilism. Seemingly to this day if you listen to some of its vote-hungry politicians.

Indeed, Dr. Greenspan says as much when noting in his memoirs that

"Current account balances refer only to transactions that cross *sovereign* borders. Our tabulations are loosely rooted in the obsession of the mercantilists of the early eighteenth century to achieve a surplus in their balance of payments that brought gold, then the measure of the wealth of a nation, into the country."[53]

What do I mean?

The **American System:**[54] (America, 1824-1945, with sporadic re-appearances to this day by various politicians) is the legacy of Alexander Hamilton's *Report on Manufacturers* in which he maintained that the US could not become totally independent until it had become self-sufficient in all necessary economic products.[55] The term was

---

[53] Greenspan, Alan, op. cit., p. 354. Dr. Greenspan makes the intriguing observation on the same page that: "Were we to measure financial net balances of much *smaller* geographic divisions, such as the individual American states…, or of much *larger* groupings of nations, such as South America or Asia, the trends in these measures and their seeming implications could be quite different from those extracted solely from the conventional sovereignty-delineated *nation* measure: the current account balance." (*Italics by the author.*)

[54] This is not to be confused with another "American System", whereby Americans at the end of the 18th Century "invented" factory production. See Boorstin, Daniel J., *The Americans: The National Experience*, Vintage Books, New York, 1965, p. 30 - 31

[55] It is fascinating that another Founding Father, Benjamin Franklin, seemingly thought exactly the opposite of what

coined by Senator Henry Clay in 1824 when he sought to distinguish it from the "British System" which promoted Smith's and Ricardo's classical, free-market economic model. This became a key tenet of the National Republican Party.[56]

The American System also can be labeled "economic nationalism" or "strategic economics" as its goal is to create economic independence for the United States. Its three fundamental policies are to
Protect industry, mainly through high import tariffs and export subsidies;
Create plenty of government investment in national infrastructures such as roads, rails, and waterways, and
Create a national bank to promote industries.

To sum up, this ends our broad overview of what drives trade. *The fact is that* comparative

---

Hamilton did, and thus railed against mercantilism. See Boorstin, Daniel J., *The Americans: The Colonial Experience*, Vintage Books, 1958, p. 156-157

[56] This rejection of free trade could have had developmental roots: only when Britain had secured its industrial supremacy did she advocate free trade in order to decimate competing industries in the US and continental Europe. America went more for "free trade" after the Second World War – once she had conquered most of its industrial competitors and virtually had monopolized major sections of manufacturing.

advantage, not currency values, is the key driver. Another point is that mercantilist policy, or economic nationalism, was embedded into the American subconscious very much from 1824 to the end of World War II, i.e., for one and a quarter centuries. That is why it reappears to this day – very much in the form of portraying America's trade deficit as a national security threat in that foreigners can pull their money out of America.

Chapter VII

Why doesn't Congress just ban the U.S. multinationals?

In Chapter 3 we showed the powerful influence that US MNCs exerts on America's total trade deficit, one that demolishes the simplistic sophistry of some US politicians who disingenuously blame only the "undervalued" exchange rate and "unfair" trade practices of "bad" foreigners – such as the Chinese today, the Japanese have been "bad" in the late 1980s.

We showed you in Chapter 3 how America's global trade surplus dwarfs her headline geographical deficit. In 2005, for instance, her global trade surplus of $2.7 trillion was five times larger than her headline geographical deficit of $714 billion

We pointed out that the reason for an ever-larger MNC-driven US trade deficit *in fact* is because of MNCs' booming overseas activities. Production and sales are twice the size of America's exports. In 2004, for instance, America exported goods and services worth $808 billion. However, its MNC overseas affiliates produced and sold goods as well as services worth $2 trillion! Meanwhile, America's successful MNCs in 2004 bought $2.3 trillion worth in inputs in their respective host countries. These were 284% larger than America's total exports of goods and services.

In theory, these goods and services could be produced in America and sold abroad, correct? In theory yes, but in practice, no. We showed in Chapter 6 that nations trade with each other because they create a win-win situation based on their respective comparative advantages in factor endowments.
But why do MNCs go abroad in the first place? In Dr. Greenspan's diction: what reduces their "home bias"?[57] Surely, they must have sound business reasons for investing heavily overseas, otherwise they just would expand at home.

Experts at the US Bureau of Economic Analysis, Raymond Mataloni and Daniel Yorgason note the following concerning US foreign direct investment overseas:

"By area, high-income countries continued to be the most popular location for new affiliates in 2004. The new affiliates in these countries accounted for 74.1% of total value added of all new affiliates and for 60.3% of the total employment of all new affiliates. *The*

---

[57] See Chapter 4 for our discussion of this concept.

longstanding tendency for US MNCs to concentrate their investments in high-income countries suggests that a key factor in the decisions of US companies about foreign locations is access to large and affluent markets; other important factors may include access to a highly trained labor force and access to supplying firms." [58]

We researched this empirically some years ago[59] by focusing on German chemical, machinery, and banking corporations. The three key reasons that these successful German firms established operations in America were to

Harness the potential of the US market

Protect one's own market position in America, and

In the case of banks, to counter the offensive of foreign banks invading Germany, and to secure ample US funding.

So, while trade is driven primarily by comparative advantage, direct investment is driven primarily by the need for customer proximity. Here is a broad overview of some of the most brilliant economists' thoughts on why companies go

---

[58] Mataloni & Yorgason, op. cit., p. 49. (*Italics by the author*)
[59] Pfeil, Enzio von, op. cit., *German Direct Investments in the United States*, JAI Press, Connecticut, 1985, page

abroad. Note that the "hallowed" exchange rate as well as trade practices as arbiters of trade balances and, therefore. of direct investment, are virtually irrelevant.

There are two principal theories of what drives direct investment. First, **Prof. Raymond Vernon's** *product cycle theory*, which states that each product/company goes through four phases:[60]
It is discovered in the domestic market;
Its successful domestic sales facilitate its exports;
As soon as exports get threatened, overseas production is established, and
Ultimately, the entire product's/company's advantages disintegrate and it dies.

Another leading thinker on direct investment is **Prof**. **Richard Caves**.[61] His *theory about horizontal direct investments* states that these are industry-specific, not country-specific. This is because products have the same characteristics and production techniques everywhere. These firms have to dominate their markets and must go overseas because their competitors pursue

---

[60] Vernon, R., *The Location of Economic Activity*, in: Dunning, J. (Ed.) Economic Analysis and Multinational Enterprise, London, England, 1974, p. 89- 114
[61] Caves, R., *Industrial Organization*, in : Dunning (Ed.): Economic Analysis and Multinational Enterprise, London, England, 1974, p. 115-146

similar strategies. In our own work, the German banks establishing overseas footholds stridently voiced this: they felt threatened by the encroachment of non-German banks on their own German territory.

Other forces driving direct investment are[62]
Resource seeking: Companies need to procure either cheaper labor or natural resources overseas, mainly in developing countries, and
Strategic asset seeking: In this case, mainly resources-based companies buy overseas in order to prevent their competitors from getting the asset.

This concludes a broad overview of why US MNCs go abroad. To reiterate what Ingo Walter said about trade, US MNCs go abroad because it pays to do so.

But, if politicians are truly concerned about America's trade deficit and if they really want to boost US employment, then why not just prohibit US corporates from going abroad, *and* why not force America's foreign affiliates to shut down their overseas operations and bring everything back onshore? That way, America would have a trade surplus of about $2 trillion and plenty of employment within a few months if they made the

---

[62] Wikipedia, *Foreign Direct Investment*

penalties for non-compliance harsh enough. Or are we missing something that certain US politicians seem to know, perhaps?

Banning US MNCs' overseas operations – overtly, or by Congress just continuing to goad foreign government hosts to US MNCs – would be nothing short of a financial "9/11" for America. In 2005, repeating points made in Chapter 3, US parent MNCs in America itself accounted for
27% of US non-government employment, or 21.5 million jobs;
17% of all private fixed investment, or $341bn;
two and a half times America's exports of goods and services by way of US MNCs' global sales and production, and
nearly 25% of America's GDP.

While reining - in MNCs and forcing them back to America might provide a quick fix for the trade "deficit" and job creation, the very reason that MNCs go abroad is to make more money by improving their competitiveness in local markets. The corollary to this is that if they were forbidden to work in overseas domestic markets and instead had to go back to exporting goods, their competitiveness and therefore ability to create jobs and incomes in America would suffer enormously. All the more so, given the shabbiness of US pre-university educational training, as well as the almost total absence of decent vocational training.

Were certain US politicians, in their quixotic mercantilist quest to create a trade surplus, to ban US MNCs' overseas operations, the other disaster would be of financial nature: The quoted shares of such companies would crash, obliterating billions of dollars worth of market capitalization on America's various exchanges. This, in turn, would hurt consumption (*inter alia*, by massacring the value of ordinary citizens' 401-Ks) and, in turn, American jobs.

Indeed, in her excellent book on China and India, Robyn Meredith points out that the two groups benefiting hugely from American companies producing in China are the consumer, who gets cheaper goods, and the corporations, whose profits are fattened by virtue of production costs being much lower in China[63] – not to mention their huge revenues generated by selling their goods *in China herself*. Indeed, this ultimately is why US MNCs' "home bias" dwindles. There is more money to be made overseas. Indeed, in early October 2007, General Electric, the world's second-largest corporation by market

---

[63] Meredith, Robyn: *The Elephant and The Dragon: The Rise of India and China and What It Means for All of Us*, W. W. Norton & Company, New York, 2007, p. 196

capitalization, announced for the first time ever that during 2007, its operations outside of America would earn it more money than its domestic US operations. Mr. Ferdinando Beccalli-Falco, head of GE's non-US operations, stated that "...business was growing at more than twice the pace of developed markets and was likely to expand 20% a year for the next several years."[64]

Finally, banning US MNCs from operating abroad would damage overseas economies as well. As pointed out by Raymond Mataloni and Daniel Yorgason in Chapter 3, US non-bank affiliates account for 15% of Ireland's, 12% of Singapore's, and 10% of Canada's GDPs.

So, the quick fix that would eliminate America's trade deficit and create many jobs – one that would presumably serve some US politicians' interests – is actually a recipe for a financial "9/11". We simply cannot understand why US MNCs, US investment banks, and US unions, should want this from those they have elected to represent their interests in Washington, D.C. What am I missing out on?

---

[64] Reuters, *GE expects sales in emerging markets to outstrip those in US,* South China Morning Post, 2nd October 2007, p. B8

But US politicians do not even *overtly* have to ban US MNCs. If certain US politicians continue antagonizing US MNCs' host countries, then what is to keep any host country from making life difficult for the overseas affiliates of these American MNCs? Maybe Congress already is angering China so much that Beijing itself turns on US firms operating in China and throws them out. Look at what Robert Mugabe has done to foreign companies operating in Zimbabwe. Such things have happened throughout history![65] If this is how certain US politicians want their MNCs treated abroad, we wonder why such MNCs even bother putting money into these politicians' campaign coffers in the first place?

---

[65] Who of us remembers Eugene Burdick's and William Lederer *The Ugly* American (W.W.Norton & Company, New York City, 1999) as an example of how Americans made themselves unpopular and thus were shunned overseas? This is not meant to be taken as anti-American. I most certainly am not; there is a great deal of "good" in America that goes unnoticed by people who have not lived extensively in America. In Eugene, Oregon, I became one of America's youngest Eagle Scout as well as God and Country recipients in the sixties: this illustrates what opportunities America offers to anyone willing to believe in himself and work hard. However, in today's world, America is "the" superpower and thus role model; hence, we have to cite America. At the end of the day, hypocrisy, expediency and thus sophistry rule any country. It's just that America is the biggest example of such egregiousness today. Sadly!

You don't need a Ph.D. in economics to figure out that if, for instance, China forbids US MNCs – including all American financial institutions – from operating in China, then all *non*-American MNCs would be thrilled. They can fill the vacuum and increase their market share in China. Is this really what US politicians want? But: how much do these *non-US* MNCs finance the campaign coffers of certain US politicians? What goal are certain US politicians doggedly pursuing by threatening the operations of the very companies who are supporting them and the US economy? In order to garner the campaign finance of non-US MNCs? Curious logic, would you not agree.

But what can be done to move the trade debate away from the sophistic appeal of "undervalued" exchange rates and "unfair" trade practices to a more mature and thus productive, 21st Century level? My suggestions revolve around:
Changing the mindset of politicians by bringing trade balance accounting into the 21st Century;
Introducing an interim tax solution to help the working classes whose educational needs have been patently ignored by many US politicians,
Lifting the quality of the US workforce by improving the vocational and pre-college education system in order to make American workers richer and thus less belligerent towards their richly - paid superiors.

1. Bring trade balance accounting into the 21st century. The headline trade balances that we all read about are based on double-entry bookkeeping. This was formalized by the Italian monk and da Vinci's friend, Luca Pacioli (1445-1517), and adopted by trade balance accounting during the era of mercantilism (1500-1750). This means that the methodology upon which trade flows are calculated is over 500 years old! Thus, while the world has built on the foundations laid by thinkers such as da Vinci, Galileo and Smith, some US politicians doggedly have clung to a framework provided by a friend of da Vinci's! Perhaps this, not that enjoyable book, should be called "The Da Vinci Code"?

To reflect the realities of globalization, *national* trade balances have to be replaced by *multinational* ones. Back to the wisdom of The Talmud: We do not see things as *they* are, but as *we* are. The 500-year-old mindset persists in excluding MNCs from trade balances. We should get the accounting method up to scratch, so that we are at least talking about current and future, not past, realities.

Knowing what we are talking about is vital from a trade angle: If certain US politicians keep thumping their mercantilist, national trade balance drum, American multinationals could start becoming the target of protectionist counter-measures by host countries. The economic consequences of such counter-measures – from rising inflation and thus interest rates, leading to more unemployment and thus understandable civil unrest – are scary from an international security angle. Historically, foreign firms have been expropriated and expelled by host countries with the attendant job losses in the local economies. Shanghai, Cuba and Zimbabwe are recent examples of such "economic warfare". [66]

Two modernizations of trade balance accounting spring to mind. The first is my own, presented in Chapter 3: Overall trade balances are replaced with trade balances arising from US MNCs' overseas activities. That way one can calculate a global trade surplus, which is about six times larger than America's headline domestic trade deficit. The global trade surplus is derived by including U.S. MNCs' overseas purchases and sales of goods and services, while the headline domestic deficit excludes any overseas activities of U.S. MNCs, focusing instead solely on what leaves and enters the shores of the United States *(Chapter 3)* and *see chart 7, Page 107.*

Another approach, advocated by the US Bureau of Economic Analysis, is the "ownership-based"

---

[66] Tzu, Sun, *The Art of War*, Translated by Samuel B. Griffith, Oxford University Press, London, 1963, p.67

framework.[67] In the ownership-based system, cash flows between US and foreign parents of MNCs are netted off against each other. For instance, net receipts of US parents of direct investment income from the sales by their foreign affiliates were $310.2 billion in 2006. Meanwhile, net payments to foreign parents of direct investment income from the sales by their US affiliates were $136.0 billion. The result is that the headline US current account deficit in goods and services of $758.5 billion in 2006 shrank by $174.2 billion, to $584.3 billion. This $174.2 billion was the net surplus in receipts collected by the parents of US MNCs from their overseas affiliates. In 2006, that net surplus reduced America's headline deficit on goods and services by 23%. *See chart 20, page 120.*

Whether you use the global approach or the ownership-based one, the mindsets of the public at large and thus of many politicians would be enlightened considerably by moving trade balance accounting into the 21st century.

2. Introduce an interim tax solution. Professors Scheve and Slaughter assert that protectionist sentiment is rearing its head again

---

[67] Lowe, Jeffrey H., *An Ownership-Based Framework of the US Current Account, 1997 – 2006*, Survey of Current Business, Washington D.C., January 2008, p. 59 - 61

because of "...the link between market performance and opinions on globalization, *and* the recent absence of real income growth for so many Americans..."[68]

They mesh stagnating income growth for the working classes with politics as follows:

"Given the lack of recent real income growth for most Americans, newfound skepticism about globalization is not without cause. Nor it is without effect: The change in public opinion is the impetus for protectionist drift in policy. Politicians have an incentive to propose and implement protectionist policies because more citizens want them, and protectionist special interests face an audience of policymakers more receptive to their lobbying effort than at any time in the last two decades. "[69]

While we join those individuals believing that the key to keeping one's comparative advantage is education, time is of the essence: "Significant payoffs from an educational investment will take decades to be realized..."[70]

---

[68] Scheve, Kenneth E. and Slaughter, Matthew J., *A New Deal for Globalization*, Foreign Affairs, July/August 2007, p. 42

[69] ibid. , p. 42

[70] ibid. , p. 42

In order to re-distribute the monetary effects of globalization as quickly and effectively as possible, they suggest that the payroll tax be removed for all workers earning below the national median of an annual $32,140. This tax cut would affect 67 million workers and would be worth $3,800 per worker. They go on to discuss the funding of this tax cut for workers.[71]

Their sensible suggestion would temper rising protectionist sentiment among those most affected, the working class, elegantly and quickly – thus creating time in which to introduce more fundamental measures such as the modernization of America's vocational as well as pre-university education, which we discuss next.

But more could be done to make America more attractive for corporations to move to or expand operations in. Recently, US Treasury Secretary Henry Paulson stated that "Uncle Sam was undermining the competitiveness of American workers."[72] Indeed, according to the same article, America's overall tax rate (i.e., if one combines state with federal taxes) is 39%, the second highest in the OECD after Japan. Meanwhile, America's effective marginal rate of 24% is the

---

[71] ibid. , p. 45
[72] Economist, The, *Tax Reform: Overhauling the old jalopy*, New York, 4th August 2007, p. 65-66

OECD's third highest, after Germany and Japan.[73] We wonder why certain members of Congress, instead of promoting protectionism with all of its disastrous results for US MNCs, have not focused on improving the business climate for the American workers and corporations by reducing taxes, etc. along the lines being suggested here? Surely this cannot be so difficult to see, can it? Why would Americans vote *against* lower taxes and less regulation and better (pre-college) education? Why would U S employers -be glad to finance the campaigns of those enlightened politicians seeking office on such 21st-century platforms? I am puzzled, are not you?

3. Improving vocational as well as pre-university education in the US. When discussing what drives trade in Chapter 6, we introduced the Heckscher-Ohlin (HO) theorem: A country has a comparative advantage in producing a certain product if it is relatively well endowed with inputs that are used intensively in producing this product. Having grown up in America, Germany and England and now viewing all three along with Asia from a Hong Kong perch, I have gone through many educational systems. My overall observation is that while America's top universities are the best in the world, its

---

[73] ibid. , p. 65

education for the public at large – particularly on the vocational as well as pre-college level – has to fill 21st Century business requirements, and this is where politicians really could help. Instead of blaming "undervalued" exchange rates and "unfair" trade practices for creating national, macro trade deficits, and making the tax as well as regulatory lives of American workers and MNCs difficult, why not take a leaf from the HO theorem and improve that one-factor endowment which desperately needs it – educating the American public at large.?[74]

Education is crucial as HO's key factor endowment because times are changing. Dr. Greenspan notes that

"A dysfunctional US elementary and secondary education system has failed to prepare our students sufficiently rapidly to prevent a shortage of skilled workers and a surfeit of lesser-skilled ones, expanding the pay gap between the two groups. Unless America's education system can raise skill levels as quickly as technology requires, skilled workers will continue to earn greater wage increases, leading to ever more disturbing extremes of income concentration."[75]

---

[74] Also see Blinder, Alan S., op. cit. , p. 4
[75] Greenspan, Alan, op. cit. , p. 505

My study of history makes me believe that just as trade protectionism breeds global wars, glaring educational and thus income disparities fuel domestic political revolutions – whether in France, Russia, China, or elsewhere.

Reverting to Dr. Greenspan's views on the need to educate skilled workers, Prof. Blinder[76] points out that the world has undergone three industrial revolutions:
The first Industrial Revolution led from the farm to the factory occurring at the same time as David Hume and Adam Smith advocated capitalism's "invisible hand" whereby market forces, not *diktat*, rule the economic evolution:
The second Industrial Revolution is still with us: jobs are moving from factories to services, and
The third Industrial Revolution, the Information Age, means that "The cheap and easy flow of information around the globe has vastly expanded the scope for tradable services."

Importantly, Prof. Blinder asserts that the first Industrial Revolution did *not* spell the end of agriculture. The number of Americans working on farms is the same today as it was in 1810, however, the *share* of agriculture's employment has fallen drastically. The second Industrial Revolution did *not* spell the end of manufacturing

---
[76] Blinder, Alan S., op. cit. , p. 5-7

either. The number of factory workers has shrunk marginally since this Revolution began, but their *share* of total employment has diminished dramatically. The share of manufacturing jobs will drop again during the third Industrial Revolution.

We would add, however, that time is increasingly of the essence. Emerging markets such as China and India are going through their first Industrial Revolutions, and the more advanced emerging markets in the rest of Asia are morphing into their second and even third Industrial Revolutions. So those politicians seriously wanting to lead America (as opposed just winning their next election) must prepare the public at large to create more employment in the Information Age. Prof. Blinder agrees that "…our education system may need to change massively."[77] To repeat: Because such changes take a long time, an interim solution is that Congress should protect America's workers and corporations by cutting taxes as suggested above. In a nutshell: Congress should cut taxes and introduce drastic changes to America's pre-university educational systems as soon as possible. Why does Congress refuse to take such simple steps – instead of threatening the existence of US MNCs and thus of US workers?

---

[77] Blinder, Alan S., op. cit., p. 9

Previously, we discussed the understandably tight linkage between education levels and protectionist sentiment. Add to this another tight linkage deduced from the HO Theorem: Because trade flows are governed by what each country is good at, its comparative advantage, the linkage between trade balances and education is tight. The better the education system for the population at large, the higher the quality and thus quantity of what a nation sells globally. This is especially true of highly industrialized economies, i.e., the ones that are not reliant on the export of natural resources. This is one reason Germany and Japan, despite rising currencies (see Chapter 2), consistently have recorded growing trade surpluses. The quality of their workforces is higher especially due to excellent vocational training.

Here are some disturbing observations about the parlous state of education for America's public at large, those to which politicians wishing to enhance American competitiveness should devote more of their energies to – instead of blaming foreigners and taxing American workers and corporations financially and educationally as well as imposing onerous regulations:

One-third of America's high school students fail to graduate, [78] not to mention America's poor record in thorough vocational training;

The US Department of Education (DOE) reckons[79] that 25 million Americans, or 8% of the population, are functionally illiterate; they cannot rely on reading as a primary source of information. Educator Chester E Finn, Jr., states, "Just five percent of seventeen-year-old high school students can read well enough to understand and use the information found in technical materials, literary essays, and historical documents. Barely six percent can solve multi-step math problems and use basic algebra";

The DOE estimates that 40 million Americans, or 13% of the population, can sign their name but cannot understand such basics as the instructions for programming a VCR, reading a map, or (how to) accurately fill out an application for a Social Security card. The National Institute for Literacy writes that "more than 60% of front-line workers in goods-producing businesses have

---

[78] Jay P. Green and Greg Forster, *Public High School Graduation and College Readiness Rates in the United States*, Education Working Paper No. 3, the Manhattan Institute, September 2003. Cited in: The Council on Foreign Relations, *US-China Relations: An Affirmative Agenda, A Responsible Course* , p. 76, 2007

[79] Stelly Sr., Timothy N., *Illiteracy in America*, Useless-Knowledge.com, 22nd August 2005, Cyberspace

difficulty applying information from a text to a required task";
A national survey taken some years ago claimed that 50% of Americans have never read a newspaper and 75% have never ventured into a bookstore. Many teachers also lack basic skills. One example is in Texas, where in 1983, 3000 teachers were required to take a competency test. More than 60% failed the reading portion, and 46% failed at math. Twenty-six percent could not pass the writing exam and to cap it all off, more than a quarter of the group cheated.

Educator Timothy Stelly's conclusion: "This inability to perform proficiently is the by-product of workers having difficulty adjusting to new demands of their jobs spawned by technological advancements." So how can America compete globally in the production of high-value goods if its very educational foundation is rotting, thereby removing its workforce's ability to globalize flexibly?

America does *not* need more college graduates. They are not the ones actually making the goods, factory workers do that. And the quality and productivity of their work needs to be improved dramatically.

Therefore, what we propose is that America introduces vocational training certificates by creating apprenticeships. Just as with America's world-class CPA and CFA certificates, workers would take courses and become, for instance, a Certified Mechanic, Certified Cook, Certified Hairdresser or Certified Carpenter. Such nation-wide training would be financed by the various industry groups or companies for whom the training is being conducted, e.g. the Mechanics Association or the Builders Association. They, in turn, would be able to claim all such expenses against their corporate taxes. That would clearly improve the US comparative advantage as regards resource endowment for 67 million workers – the very people to whom "...the benefits of integration have been unevenly distributed."[80]

The OECD, in May 2007,[81] addressed the issue of globalization and provided various policy recommendations, *inter alia*
"Enhancing potential job creation and labor market adjustment
 greater product market competition
 reduced employment protection legislation
 education / training policies to equip workers with general skills

---

[80] ibid. , p. 38
[81] Pain, Nigel and Koske, Isabell, *The Effects of Globalization on Labor Markets, Productivity and Inflation*, OECD, Paris, 15th June 2007, p. 27

But there is another reason for emphasizing that American public education has to improve – and quickly: "Research on polling data shows that opinions about trade, FDI and immigration are closely correlated to skill and educational levels. Less skilled Americans – who make up the majority of the US labor force – have long led opposition to open borders. Workers with only high school educations are almost twice as likely to support protectionist policies as works with college educations are.[82]

When discussing America's third Industrial Revolution, Prof. Blinder makes another valuable point:[83]

"Some types of work are easily deliverable down an electronic wire.... with little or no diminution in quality, and some are not. This unconventional divide, I believe, will prove to be the critical labor market division in the future. The interesting thing is that it does *not* correspond at all well to traditional distinctions between jobs that require high levels of education and jobs that do not...The dividing line between jobs that are suitable for electronic delivery (and thus are threatened by offshoring) and those that are not does not correspond to traditional distinctions

---

[82] Scheve and Slaughter, op. cit., p. 39
[83] Blinder, Alan S., op. cit., p. 9

between high-end and low-end work. And that is why more education, full stop, cannot be the answer. "

So, beyond purely vocational training, the author's own experience in American grade schools, junior high, and high schools and then returning to Germany to do the *Abitur* (equivalent to English A-Levels or the French Baccalaureate) has left him with the deep impression that public, pre-university education in America leaves plenty of scope for modernization, too. As Robyn Meredith notes in her recent book[84]: "Just when the United States should be beefing up its educational system, voters have tolerated...the failure of many public school systems to educate students even at a basic level year after year after year."

So how should America's public pre-university education be modernized in Friedman's globalized flat world? He suggests that the following skills be honed especially among the working classes so that they can benefit from global flattening:[85] by producing goods and services that cannot be made better or more cheaply abroad. He calls people with such skill sets "untouchables".

---

[84] Meredith, Robyn, op. cit., p. 190
[85] Friedman, op. cit., p. 285 - 307

"Great collaborators and orchestrators" are those who can run and orchestrate 24/7/7 supply chains, i.e., 24 hours a day, seven days a week, and over seven continents;

"The great explainers" are those who can exercise perspicacity by simplifying the complex, the more inter-connected our globe becomes;

The great leveragers" are people who can leverage technology so that others can work smarter and faster, thus competing with cheaper foreign labor by increasing productivity and thus by reducing unit labor costs;

"The great adapters" are like Swiss army knives; they are versatile and can carry out a number of functions;

"The green people" are going to be involved in a huge industry involving the words "sustainable" and "renewable", e.g. renewable energy, and sustainable development;

"The passionate personalizers" are those who can take ordinary service jobs and give them a very personal touch so that people will want those services, and

"The math lovers" are those who can apply mathematics in order to speed things up. Friedman notes: "In 62% of American jobs over the next ten years, entry-level workers will need to be proficient in algebra, geometry, data interpretation, probability and statistics."[86], and "The great localizers" are "...those small and medium-sized firms that learn how to take all the global capabilities that are now out there and tailor them to the needs of the local community. It's the localization of the global..."[87]

There you have it. Globalization has left trade balances behind. The framework and "software" used to measure trade balances is over five centuries old from an accounting as well as from a (mercantilist/American System) mindset. Many politicians are basing their sophistry on vestigial trade myths that are dangerously irrelevant and could lead to catastrophic military consequences that we have seen before. They are ignoring MNCs at their peril when studying trade flows and subsequently bellowing about trade policy. Can we not all learn from the mistakes of history?

Finally, the only way for America to improve its trade balances is to factor MNC trade flows into the equation, slash taxes for the working classes so that they benefit from globalization, lower corporate taxes, sharply streamline America's onerous regulatory regime for its MNCs and other

---

[86] Friedman, op. cit. He is citing a study released by the American Diploma Project, p. 302
[87] ibid. , citing IBM strategist Joel Cauley, p. 303

companies, and improve its vocational and all pre-university education drastically so that everyone has a chance to prosper during global flattening.

Arnold Toynbee, having studied the rise and fall of all civilizations and discussing the virtues of adversity, concluded that it is not what happened to them, but *how they reacted to what happened*, that made them great or mediocre. To repeat his statement: "…in the geneses of civilizations, the interplay between challenges and responses is *the* factor which counts above all…"[88] America's politicians stand at such a crossroads. As Toynbee pointed out, habits can be changed, including those of the mindset that was framed by the 16th century trade accountant, Luca Pacioli.

Prof. Boorstin, a great immigrant from Germany, wrote the following about Americans:

" 'Discontent, Oscar Wilde once observed, 'is the first step in the progress of a man or a nation.' This is surely true today. Our problem is complicated by the fact that the prescriptions, which nations offer for themselves, are also symptoms of their diseases. But illusory solutions

---

[88] Toynbee, Arnold, *A Study of History*, Abridgement of Volumes I - VI by D.C. Somervell, Oxford University Press, New York, Oxford, 1957, p. 76. (*Italics by the author*)

will not cure our illusions. Our discontent begins by finding false villains whom we can accuse of deceiving us. Next we find false heroes whom we expect to liberate us. The hardest, most discomfiting discovery is that each of us must emancipate himself. Each of us must disenchant himself, must moderate his expectations, must prepare himself to receive messages coming in from the outside...We should seek new ways of letting messages reach us; from our own past, from God, from the world which we may hate or think we hate. To give visas to strange and alien and outside notions. Notions of which neither we nor the Communists have ever dreamed and which we can never see in our mirror. One of our grand illusions is the belief in a 'cure'. There is no cure. There is only the opportunity for discovery. For this the New World gave us a grand, unique beginning."[89]

To sum up, it is hoped that responsible US politicians will heed Prof. Boorstin's wisdom. There is still time to show true leadership by transforming mindsets about America's trade balances and trade policies. *The fact is that* recognizing that the US itself is the largest stakeholder in the globalized economy will be the necessary first step in the process.

---

[89] Boorstin, Daniel J., *The Image: A Guide to Pseudo-Events in America*, Athenum, New York, 1975, p. 260-261

Chapter VIII

Ignore MNCs at your policy peril

This Chapter was written around the time of two historical events: Cuba was celebrating the 50th anniversary of her revolution and Pres. Obama was inaugurated while the world economy kept sliding into deeper recession.

The significance of this confluence is startling: Castro deposed American-backed dictator Batista and subsequently expropriated MNCs operating in Cuba. With the Economic Time™ worsening in America, Pres. Obama will have to deal with the vested interests of local constituents clamouring for more protection from imports. But this clamouring will not be confined only to Americans. As all politics are local, you also will read even more of swelling social unrest everywhere – with calls for protectionism getting ever more strident. After all, everybody gets to blame "the foreigner", right?

Hitherto, "protectionism" has taken two forms. The first one has been outright expropriation of MNCs, as in the case of Cuba in 1959. Such expropriation followed in the wake of an overall political earthquake. And everyone knows about the second form of protectionism: making it tougher if not downright impossible to import goods from abroad. The Smoot-Hawley Act has to be the crassest example of this trade protectionism.

Everyone knows that yesterday's Cuba is today's Zimbabwe, and that yesterday's Smoot-Hawley is being replayed today in more subtle ways of impeding imports, so we need not bore you with examples. Suffice it to say that protectionism rises when the economy falls. This is precisely where we are at again.

Having brought trade balance accounting into the 21st Century by including MNCs in the global calculation, this opens three other angles. *Firstly*, the likely emergence of "host country protectionism". *Secondly*, the very basic question: why should MNCs be financing the campaigns of those very politicians who are giving rise to host country protectionism? And *thirdly*: everybody loses even more under host country protectionism than under conventional trade protectionism.

In the language of multinationals, "host countries" are those places in which MNCs operate, for instance a U.S. bank affiliate operating in France or a Japanese car manufacturer operating in America. Of course, as we noted in our

Foreword to the Second Edition, however, "host countries" are any places in which people not "belonging" to that country operate: an American media consultant in South Africa, or a German specialty chemical purchaser in Malaysia are fictitious examples. So when we refer to "MNCs", we are referring not only to the big "name brand" multinationals that we all know of, but also of foreigners running their businesses in host countries.

By "host country protectionism" we mean that local officials or politicians in such host countries make the lives of these MNCs difficult *because of domestic politics where the MNCs are headquartered*. All readers will recall examples of local governments inflicting their wrath on the local operations of MNCs which they host, so we need not take your time by reviewing examples.[90] These peoples' motivations are manifold, but all boil-down to one thing: self-interest, whether of financial or of political nature.

But the *reason* for them taking out their wrath may shift. In earlier times, reasons revolved around: changed governments, such as the case

---

[90] Gladwin, Thomas N., and Walter, Ingo, *Multinationals Under Fire: Lessons in the Management of Conflict*, John Wiley and Sons, New York, 1980

of Cuba. Or around locals being angered at the very MNC itself, such as foreign agriculture and fruit companies in the 1950s. But this time we may see a different motivation ricochet into a backlash.

Step in host country protectionism. Here is a fictitious example. In host country X a local politician or official is irked by how the politicians back in the parent country of the MNC's headquarters are "attacking" their country. A concrete scenario might revolve around some legislators forcing the Chinese to revalue their RMB yet again; this ricochets in that the local Chinese party official makes the life of the local U.S. MNC's operation more difficult. Both the politician in the MNC's home country as well as the local party official is driven by self-interest. Of course, the only "winner" would be that MNC's local competitors, who increase their market share. Such winners include domestic companies producing a similar product or service – or the local operations of yet another country's, e.g. Italy's, MNC operating in the neighbourhood.

We are not implying that host countries always hold a gun to the head of foreigners' operations in their country. After all, as pointed out in Chapter III, U.S. non-bank affiliates account for 15% of Ireland's, 12% of Singapore's, and for 10% of Canada's respective GDPs. It hardly would be in the interest of host countries to jeopardize this employment created by foreigners operating within their shores, would it? Besides, MNCs inject other huge benefits to local economies. Next to technology transfer, these foreigners introduce competition to the local markets. Nevertheless, as all politics are local, self-interest can prevail – particularly during economic downturns such as the global Economic Clock™ currently is heralding.

Having outlined the threat of host country protectionism, this begs the second issue meriting discussion. Why should MNCs be financing the campaigns of those very politicians who are giving rise to such host country protectionism? A quick scan through the internet suggests that a great deal of America's finance is conducted by companies with a large or small international presence. We need not elaborate on this point, as readers readily will grasp what we are talking about.

Finally, who wins if the foreigner's operations in the host country are hurt by host country officials or politicians? Nobody. Just two paragraphs ago, we reviewed how important foreign MNCs are to the GDPs of various host countries' economies. Perhaps of even greater importance is just how important MNCs are to America's economy itself.

Repeating some observations from Chapter III, in America, her MNCs
employ over 30 million people, or over one quarter of the non-government labour force
account for over 40% of global revenues, and
account for nearly 25% of GDP originating in all private, non-bank U.S. businesses.

To sum up, if MNCs are ignored when crafting today's trade policy, this most likely will activate host country protectionism where they have their overseas operations. *The fact is that* such host country protectionism imperils not only geo-political relations with the host country, but also major portions of America's economic well-being itself. So why should MNCs which to finance the campaigns of politicians goading such host country protectionism?

Graphs, Facts and Challenges

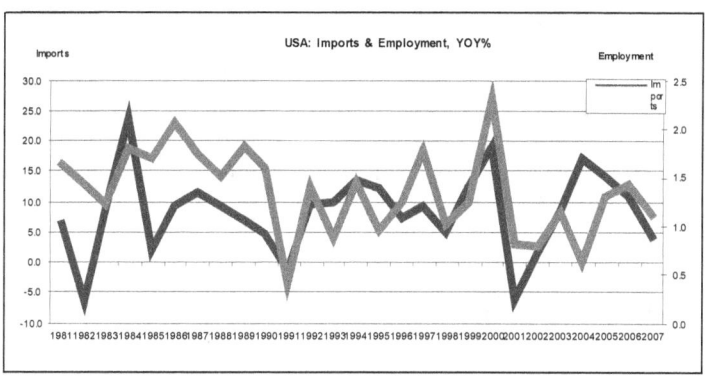

Chart 1. *Fact:* for the past quarter of a century, imports and employment have gone hand in hand, according to The Economic Time™ in America: when America's Economic Time improves, up goes demand, so imports and jobs increase. How, then, can some politicians claim that when imports go up, jobs are destroyed?

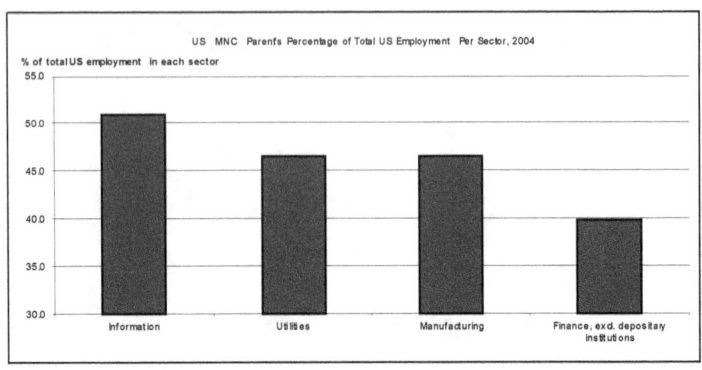

Chart 2. *Fact:* In 2004,[91] US parent MNCs accounted for 40%+ of total US employment in the sectors shown in the chart above. These employed 21.2 million people. Within manufacturing, they accounted for the following shares of employment: chemicals (100%); petroleum and coal (94%); transportation equipment (79.8%); computers and electronic products (69%); electrical equipment (56.1%), paper (57%), as well as food, beverage and tobacco (51.9%). How, then, can some politicians act as if America's very own international companies are irrelevant to US trade flows and thus to job security in America herself?

---

[91] This is when the last comprehensive survey was conducted by the Bureau of Economic Analysis

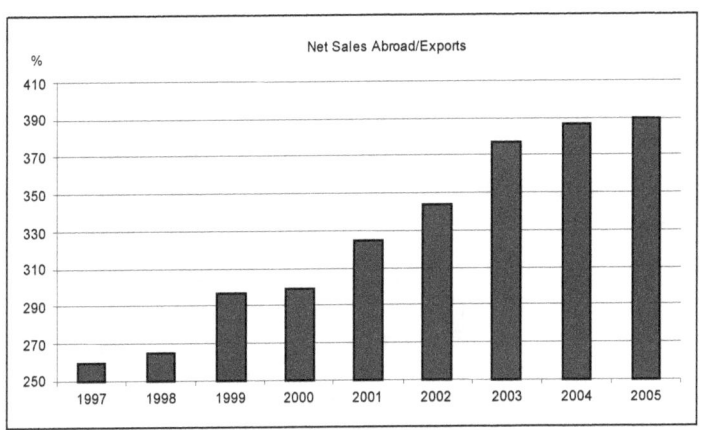

Chart 3. *Fact:* between 1997, net sales of American foreign affiliates in their host countries were over two and a half times larger than America's exports of goods and services. By 2005, they were nearly four times the size of total exports. How, then, can some politicians decry "bad" foreigners for creating America's "bad" deficit when in fact her very own companies are responsible for this development?

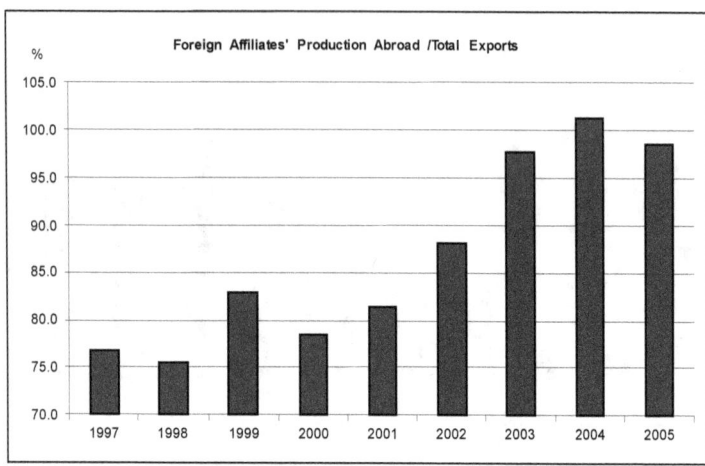

Chart 4. *Fact:* On average, the foreign affiliates of US multinationals produce nearly as much overseas as America exports in goods and services. How, then, can some politicians argue that America's deficit is "bad" and thus requires American retaliation because of "unfair" treatment by foreigners?

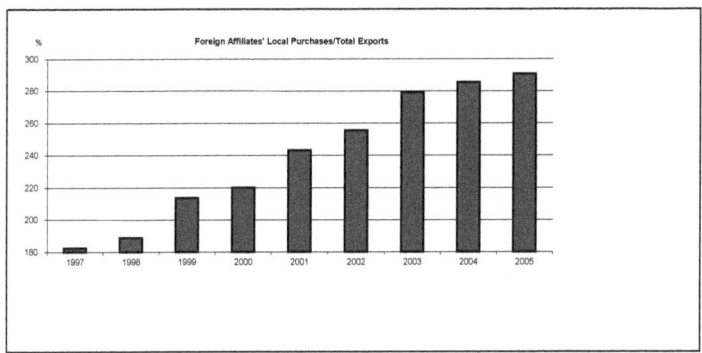

Chart 5. *Fact*: on average, the foreign affiliates of U.S. MNCs buy nearly two and half times as much in their host countries as America exports by way of goods and services. Surely these MNCs are buying inputs in their host countries in order to generate profits that subsequently benefit American shareholders and secure American jobs. How, then, can some politicians argue against their very own MNCs' overseas successes?

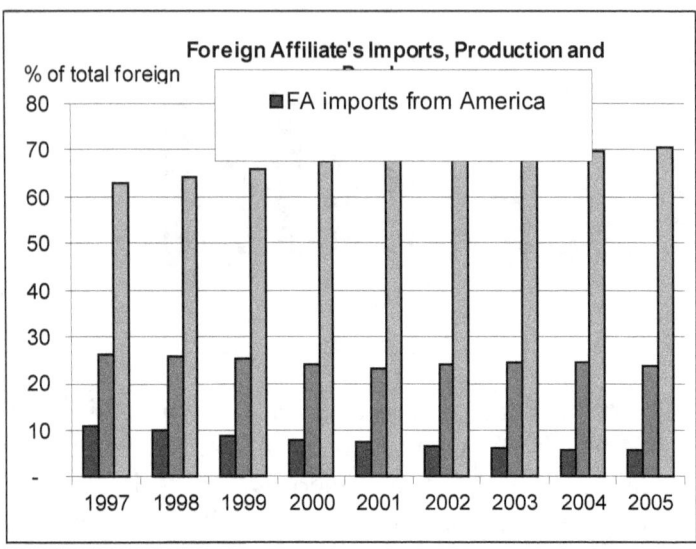

Chart 6. *Fact:* On average, foreign affiliates' local purchases in their host countries account for 68% of total sales, while their local production in their host countries accounts for another 25% of sales. Their imports from America constitute a mere eight percent of the total, and this share is dwindling at the expense of increased local purchases. How, then, can some politicians argue that foreigners are being "unfair" when, in fact, U.S. overseas affiliates are buying more and more in their overseas host countries?

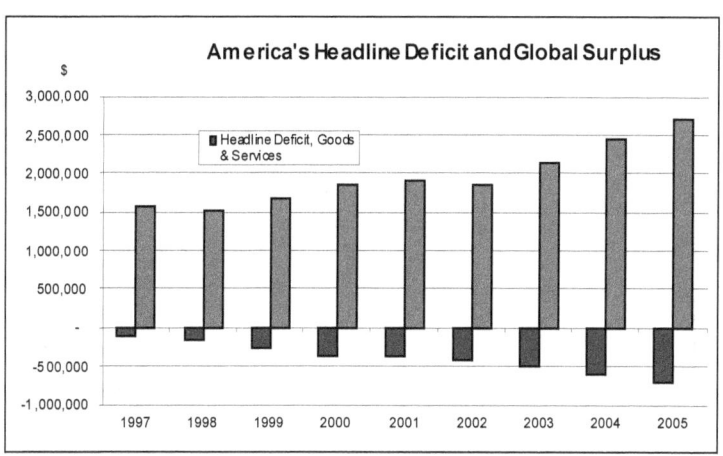

Chart 7. *Fact:* on average, America's global trade surplus is four times the size of her headline, geographical deficit. In 2005, for instance, her global trade surplus of $2.7 trillion dwarfed her headline geographical deficit of $714 billion. *How, then, can some politicians* disingenuously disregard the success of their very own MNCs' global operations, instead using 15th century software from which to garner votes cheaply today?

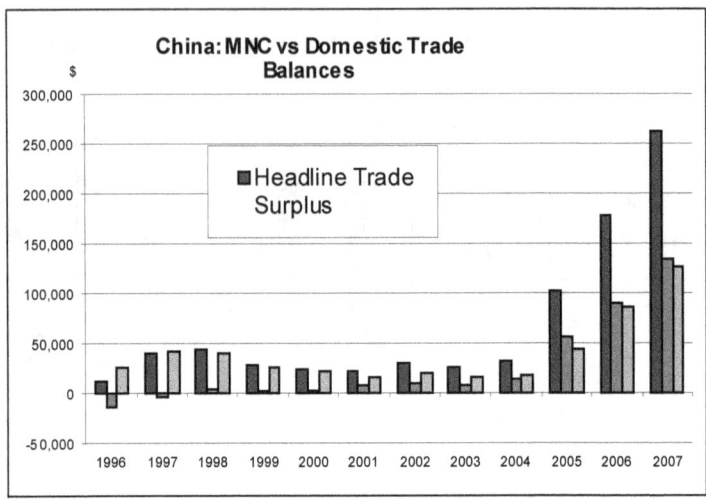

Chart 8. *Fact:* from 1997 - 2007, MNCs' share of China's headline geographical trade surplus has rocketed nearly eight-fold, from 6.6% to 51.5%. How, then, can some politicians blame China for her trade surplus – when it is America's very own companies who increasingly are responsible for China's growing trade surplus?

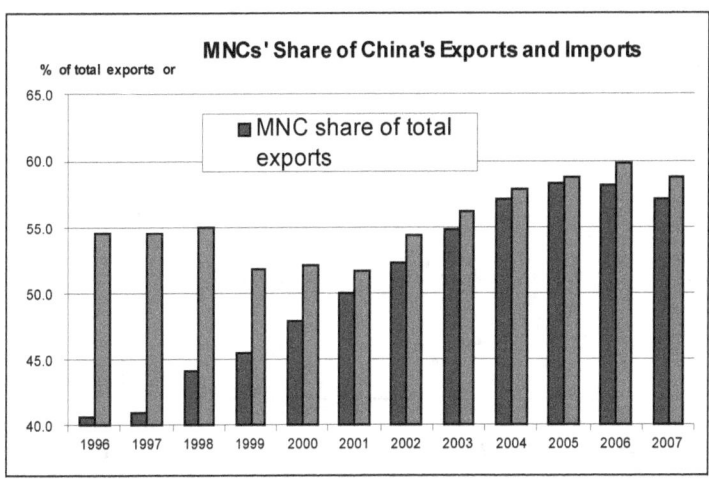

Chart 9. *Fact*: since 1996, all MNCs' share of China's exports has jumped from 41%, to 57% of total exports. How, then, can some politicians claim that China's trade surplus is created by Chinese companies – when their very own MNCs so overtly determine China's exports?

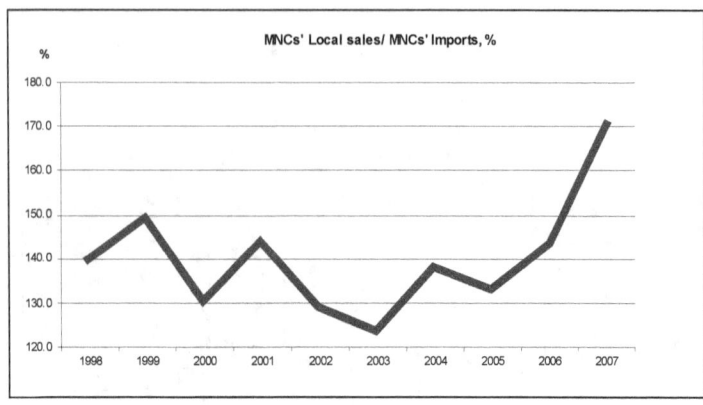

Chart 10. *Fact:* in 1998, the domestic sales of all MNCs operating in China were $107 billion, while their imports were $77 billion; thus, their local sales equated to 140% of their imports. A decade later, their local sales stood at $955 billion, while their own imports were $561 billion, meaning that their local sales equated to 170% of their own imports. How, then, can some politicians bemoan China's purported surplus when it is their very own MNCs who are electing to make and sell goods domestically in China – instead of importing them from where the parent company resides and these politicians rule?

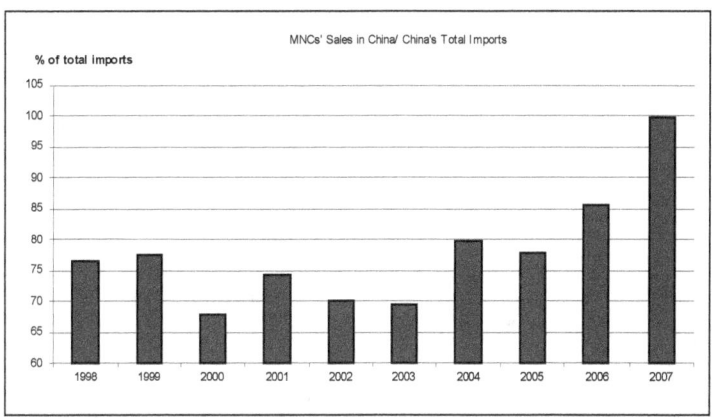

Chart 11. *Fact:* between 1998 – 2007, the ratio of what all MNCs sold domestically to China's total imports jumped by one third, from 77% to 100%. In other words, were there no MNCs producing and selling in China, her imports would have to have doubled in 2007 in order to replace domestically-sold goods. How, then, can some politicians blame Chinese companies for creating a surplus when, in fact, their very own overseas affiliates are doing this by virtue of producing in China herself – instead of importing from the MNC parents' overseas home countries?

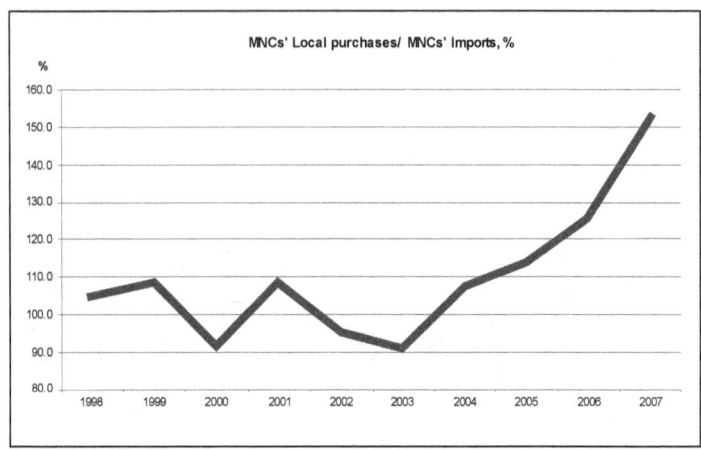

Chart 12. *Fact*: in 1998, the local production of MNCs operating in China was $80 billion, while their imports were $77 billion; thus, their local production equated to 104% of their imports. A decade later, their local production stood at $856 billion, while their own imports were $561 billion, meaning that their local production equated to 153% of their imports. How, then, can some politicians bemoan China's purported surplus when it is their very own MNCs who are electing to produce domestically in China herself – instead of importing from where the parent company resides?

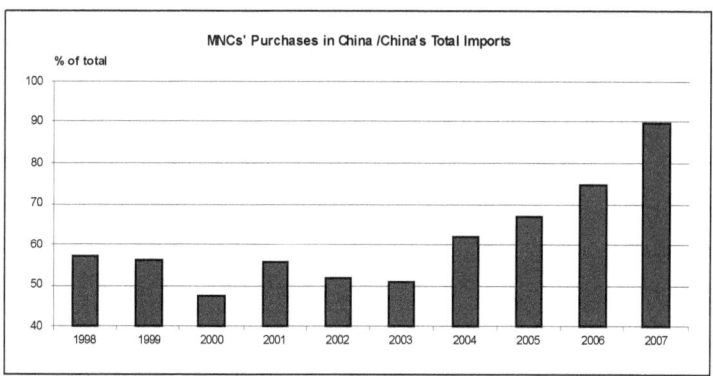

Chart 13. *Fact*: between 1998 – 2007, the ratio of all MNCs' local production in China to her total imports rocketed by nearly two thirds, from 57% to 90%. In other words, were these MNCs barred from purchasing goods in China, her imports nearly would have doubled. How, then, can some politicians berate the Chinese when it is their very own companies who are electing to produce in China itself – instead of importing them from where the MNCs are headquartered?

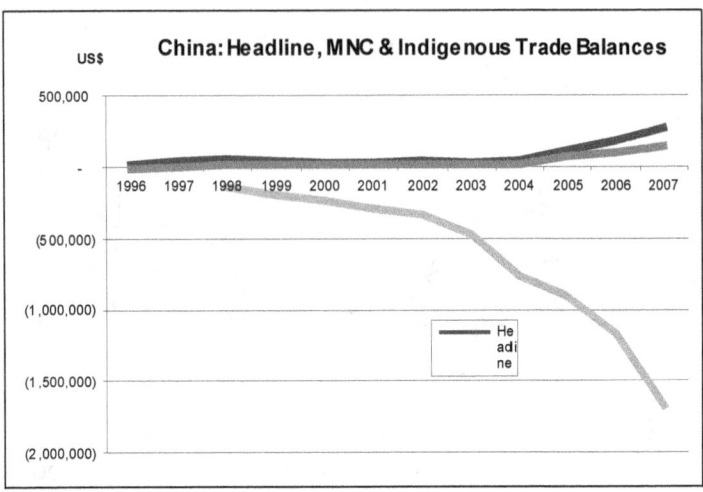

Chart 14. *Fact*: in 2007, China's global trade deficit of $1.7 trillion was over six times larger in absolute terms than her headline geographical surplus of $264 billion. How, then, can some politicians insist on ignoring the power of MNCs when debating trade issues?

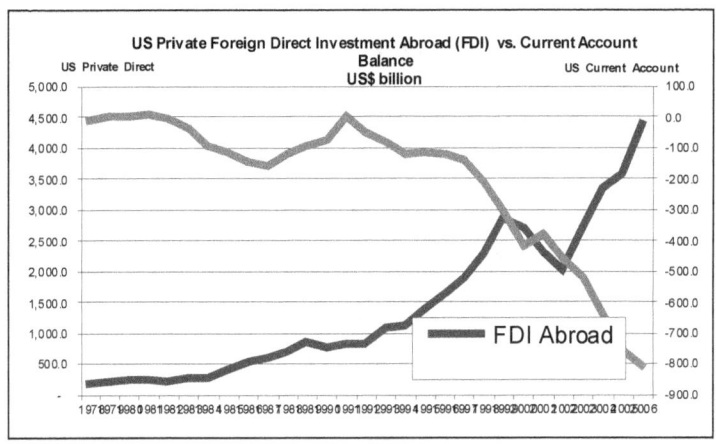

Chart 15. *Fact:* Especially as of 1990, US MNCs started investing significantly overseas - thus diminishing Dr. Greenspan's "home bias". That went hand-in-hand with a sharp deterioration of America's geographical current account balance – courtesy of what we discussed in Chapter 3. How, then, can some politicians claim that America's trade deficit is only due to "bad" foreigners with "undervalued" exchange rates and "unfair" trade practices – while ignoring the very successes of their own MNCs' overseas operations?

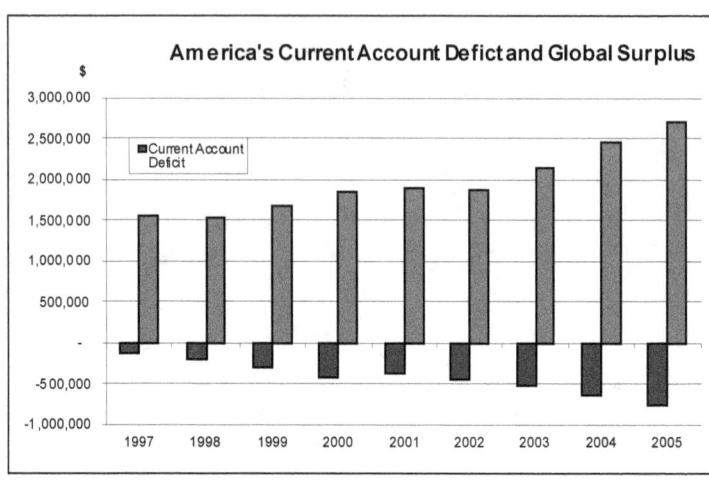

Chart 16. *Fact*: In 2005, America had a geographical current account deficit of $714 billion – but a global trade surplus was $2.7 trillion. How, then, can some politicians claim that America's savings are lower than what they are when, in reality, America's very own MNCs are generating huge surpluses that are nearly five times the size of the her current account deficit? Just because these savings are not located in America does not make them un-American, do they? Surely a great deal of such US savings are held abroad, for instance, in tax shelters – legally avoiding taxes created by some politicians who are ranting about China's "unfair" trade surplus...

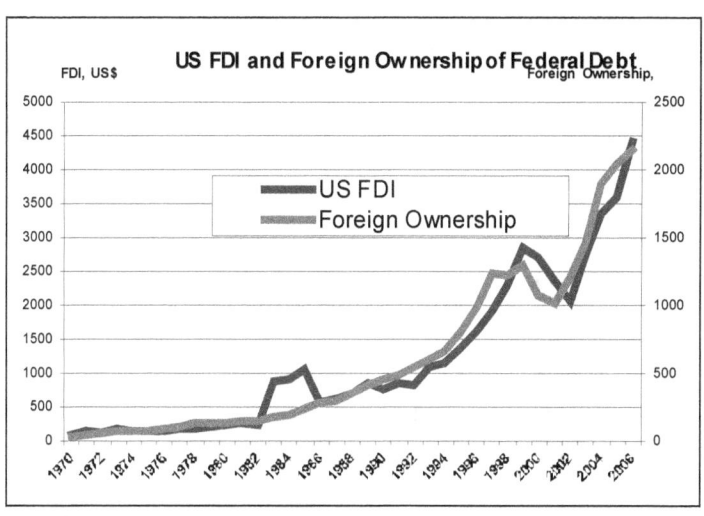

Chart 17. *Fact:* The more America invests abroad, the stronger the foreign private ownership of US debt, including that held by US MNCs operating worldwide.92 How, then, can some politicians maintain that foreign governments want to hold America's finances hostage, when a substantial chunk of foreigners' holdings of US federal debt is probably owned by US corporations (MNCs and hedge funds, etc.) enjoying legitimate tax havens? In this context, who is a "foreign" holder of US debt?

---

[92] Council of Economic Advisers, op. cit., various years, "International Investment Position of the U.S. at year-end". Foreign ownership: Office of the Management and Budget, *Foreign ownership of US Treasury securities: Analytical Perspectives*, Fiscal Year 2006, Table 16-6, p. 258

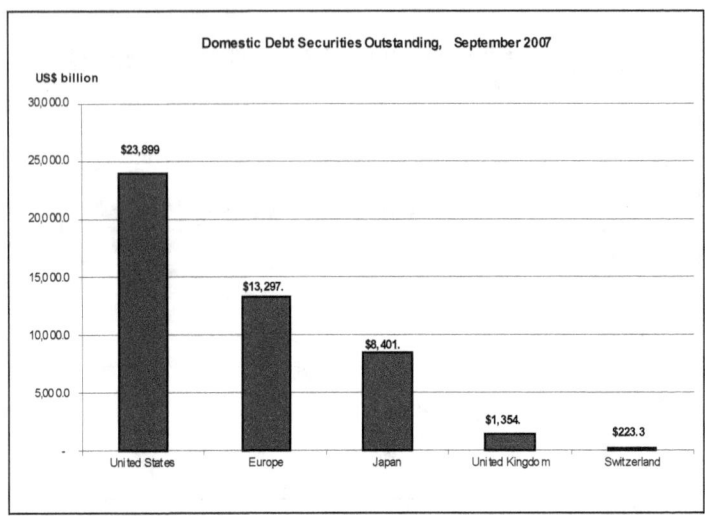

Chart 18. *Fact*: America's domestic bond market is larger than all of the other major ones combined. How, then, can some politicians seriously claim that foreign investors have "choices" regarding where they could park their large amounts of money, should they pull out of US capital markets?

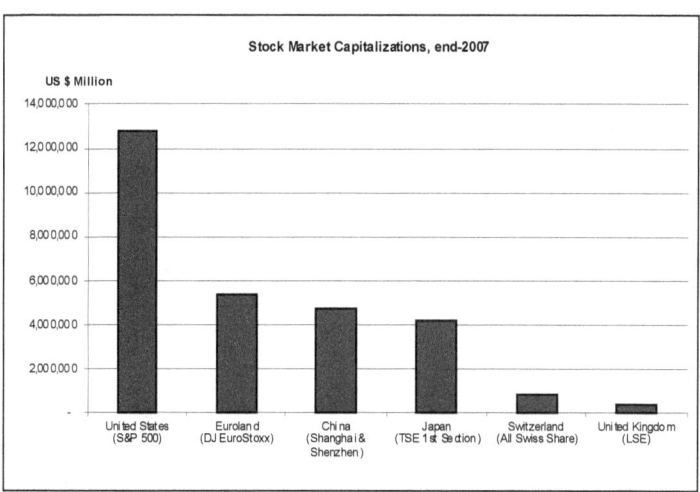

Chart 19. *Fact:* America's stock markets are bigger than all of the other major ones combined. How, then, can some politicians seriously say that foreign investors have "choices" regarding where they could park their large amounts of money, should they pull out of America's capital markets? Where could they go with all of that money, instead?

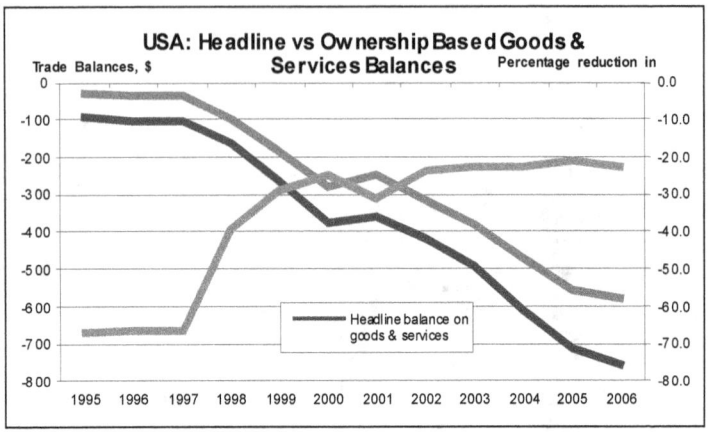

Chart 20. *Fact:* In 2006, America's headline deficit on goods and services was $758.5 billion. However, US parent MNCs received $174.2 billion in net receipts from the sales of their overseas affiliates. Thus, America's deficit on goods and services was reduced to $584.3 billion, i.e., by 23%. How, then, can some politicians claim that America's "true" trade surplus is rising when, in fact, American MNCs' overseas operations are prospering?

Acknowledgements

I owe many people my deepest appreciation for making this book possible: first and foremost, my adored and respected wife, Elizabeth, who has the tenacity to put up with a consistently temperamental and iconoclastic husband. My broking and television career would have gone nowhere without the judicious speech and debate coaching of my most influential high school teacher in Eugene, Oregon, in the 1960s: Mrs. Nancy Rose. A huge thanks also to Dr. Dirk Brandis, who made me start thinking at the kitchen table in my flat in Stadtstrasse 34, Freiburg i. Br., Germany, over 30 years ago about multinational corporations, and to Johannes Schoeter for his consistent encouragement in Hong Kong.

Then on the professional side, thanks go to my friends at Smith New Court Far East who allowed me to work with the concept of MNC trade balances when covering Japan for us in 1987 – particularly Philip Kay, who got me into the fascinating world of City broking, Michael Hope-Lewis, whose curiosity and artistic creativity with clients propelled mine, and to Angus Baxter, my best boss ever. Albert Fan and Agnes Kwan at CEIC Data have been consistently positive and gracious to me over the decades in Hong Kong.

On the research and writing side, Raymond J. Mataloni, Jr. of the Bureau of Economic Analysis was most helpful at patiently teaching me specific concepts used by his Bureau when analyzing the activities of American Multinationals. Mary Gorman Barker was kind enough to contribute her experience, brains, and diplomatic skills taming a raging bull. A special word of thanks to David Ketchum of Upstream Asia, who over only one introduction graciously gave his time to get the right spin on this book. Dr. Lee Sands was has been instrumental in that he was able to convey to me his hugely valuable political experiences as the US Trade Representative who negotiated China's WTO accession with Wu Yi. Prof. Arthur Laffer has been a refreshing post-Hayekian friend who keeps up the flag of free market economics, and Dr. Horace Brock always has inspired me in his 22nd-century economic thinking. Special are due to to V.G. Kulkarni, Anna Healy Fenton, and Alan Sargent for their help in editing and formatting, John Berthelsen for his enormous support and counsel, Alice Martell of The Martell Agency for her wisdom in navigating me through the traditional publishers' maze, and Peter Gordon for initiating me into the fascinating "new world" of online publishing in the First Edition.

For this second and new, revised edition, I am indebted to the wisdom and know-how which Joan Foo Mahony has provided in creating the new hard copy as well as the e-book edition. Another huge thanks goes to Nancy Hernreich-Bowen and to Louis Bowen for helping me to convey more effectively this book's key message – ignore MNCs at your policy peril.

Finally, I would like to thank sincerely all the special individuals who indeed have enhanced this book's credibility by endorsing it at the front of this second edition.

Being an iconoclast, all mistakes are proudly my own. As Prof. Karl Popper taught, all views are right until they are proved wrong. Put more perceptively by my respected mother-in-law, Helen Zimmern: "I know my view, so tell me yours."

Enzio von Pfeil, Hong Kong, Chinese New Year, 2009

Bibliography

Bank for International Settlements, *Quarterly Review*, Basle, Switzerland, December 2007

Blinder, Alan S., *Fear of Offshoring*, CEPS Working Paper No. 119, December 2005, Princeton University

Boorstin, Daniel J, *The Americans: The Colonial Experience*, Vintage Books, 1958
---*The Americans: The National Experience*, Vintage Books, New York, 1965, p. 30 - 31
---The Image: A Guide to Pseudo-Events in America, Atheneum, New York, 1975

Burdick, Eugene and Lederer, William, *The Ugly American*, W.W.Norton & Company, New York City, 1999

Bureau of Economic Analysis, Summary Estimates for Multinational Companies: Employment, Sales, and Capital Expenditures for 2005, Washington, D.C., 19th April 2007

Business Week, Going Ever More Global: More of the S%P 500's revenues are coming from overseas. But international diversification still pays, 20th July 2007

Caves, R., *Industrial Organization*, in: Dunning (Ed.): Economic Analysis and Multinational Enterprise, London, England, 1974

CEIC Data Ltd., Hong Kong

Council of Economic Advisers, *Economic Report of the President, various years*, Washington, D.C

Dept. of the Treasury, Federal Reserve Bank of New York, Board of Governors of the Federal Reserve System: *Report on Foreign Portfolio Holdings of US Securities, various years*

DTV *Atlas zur Musik*, Band 1, Deutscher Taschenbuchverlag/Baerenreiter Verlag Muenchen, 1977

Economist, The, *Pocket World in Figures*, London, 2007 edition
---, Tax Reform: Overhauling the old jalopy, New York, 4th August 2007

Federal Reserve Board's *Flows of Funds* data, New York, various years

Feldstein, Martin, *Why is the Dollar So High?* NBER Working Paper 13114, Cambridge, Mass., May 2007

Friedman, Thomas L., *The World is Flat*, Penguin Books, London, 2006

Gat, Azar, *The Return of Authoritarian Great Powers*, Foreign Affairs, New York, July/August 2007,

Gladwin, Thomas N., and Walter, Ingo, *Multinationals Under Fire: Lessons in the Management of Conflict*, John Wiley and Sons, New York, 1980

Green, Jay P. and Forster, Greg, *Public High School Graduation and College Readiness Rates in the United States*, Education Working Paper No. 3, the Manhattan Institute, September 2003. Cited in: The Council on Foreign Relations, *US-China Relations An Affirmative Agenda, A Responsible Course*, New York City, 2007

Greenspan, Alan, *The Age of Turbulence: Adventures in a New World*, The Penguin Press, New York, 2007

Hayek, Friedrich A. von, *Die Verhaengnisvolle Anmassung: Die Irrtuemer des Sozialismus*, Walter Eucken Institut, Freiburg i. Br., JCB More (Paul Siebeck), Tuebingen, Germany, 1996

Hildesheimer, Wolfgang, *Mozart*, Suhrkamp Verlag, Frankfurt a. M., 1977

Kagan, Robert, Of Paradise and Power: America and Europe in the New World Order, Vintage Books, 2004, New York

Kaiser, Joachim, *Erlebte Musik – von Bach bis Strawinsky*, Hoffmann und Campe, Hamburg, 1977

Kant, Immanuel, *Zum Ewigen Frieden*, Koenigsberg, 1795

Lakoff, George, Don't Think of an Elephant: Know Your Values and Frame the Debate, Chelsea Green Publishing, Vermont, 2004

Peters, Arno, *Synchronoptische Weltgeschichte:Zeitatlas*,Universum Verlag Muenchen-Solln

Lowe, Jeffrey H., *An Ownership-Based Framework of the US Current Account, 1995 – 2005*, Survey of Current Business, Washington, D.C., January 2007

Mataloni Jr., Raymond J & Yorgason, Daniel R., *Operations of US Multinational Companies: Preliminary Results from the 2004 Benchmark Survey*, Survey of Current Business, Washington, D.C., November 2006

Meredith, Robyn: The Elephant and The Dragon: The Rise of India and China and What It Means for All of Us, W. W. Norton & Company, New York, 2007

Niven, David, The Moon's A Balloon, Penguin Books, London, 1971

Office of the Management and Budget, Foreign ownership of US Treasury securities: Analytical Perspectives, Washington, D.C., various years

Pain, Nigel and Koske, Isabell, The Effects of Globalization on Labor Markets, Productivity and Inflation, OECD, Paris, 15th June 2007

Peters, Arno, *Synchronoptische Weltgeschichte: Zeitatlas*, Universum Verlag Muenchen-Solln, 1970

Pfeil, Enzio Graf von, Deutsche Direktinvestitionen in den USA: Aussagen von 76 Chemie-, Maschinenbau- und Bankgesellschaften, Fritz Knapp Verlag, Frankfurt, 1981
--German Direct Investments in the United States, JAI Press, Connecticut, 1985
---Effective Control of Currency Risks: A Practical, Comprehensive Guide, Macmillan, London, 1988
---, *Japan: Foreign Producers in Japan and the Trade Balance, 1965 – 1983*, Asia Watch, Smith New Court Far East Ltd., London, February and March 1987.
----, On China's trade balance: *Whose Surplus is it Anyway? Globalization has left trade balances behind*, Singapore Straits Times editorial, 18th November 2006
---www.EconomicClock.com, cyberspace, unrelenting

Popper, Karl R., *The Logic of Scientific Discovery*, Harper Torchbooks, New York, 1959
---, *Logik der Forschung*, 8. Auflage, J.C.B. Mohr (Paul Siebeck), Tuebingen, 1984

Riemann, Musik Lexikon, *Cantus firmus*, Sachteil, B. Schott's Soehne, Mainz, 1967

Roll, Eric Lord, *A History of Economic Thought*, Fifth Edition, Faber and Faber, London, 1992

Scheve, Kenneth and Slaughter, Matthew J., *A New Deal for Globalization*, Foreign Affairs, New York City, July/August 2007

Smith, Adam, *The Wealth of Nations*, edited by Andrew Skinner, Penguin Books, London, 1976

Spengler, Oswald, *Der Untergang des Abendlandes*, Verlag C.H. Beck, Muenchen, 1990

Standard & Poor's Equity Research, in Business Week's The Outlook, *Going Ever More Global*, 20th July 2007, New York City

Stanton, Elizabeth; Foreign US Notes Rise to 80 Percent; Treasuries Irresistible, Bloomberg.com, 6th June 2007

Stelly Sr., Timothy N., *Illiteracy in America*, Useless-Knowledge.com, Cyberspace, 22nd August 2005

Toynbee, Arnold, *A Study of History*, Abridgement of Volumes I - VI by D.C. Somervell, Oxford University Press, New York, Oxford, 1957

---, Change and Habit: The Challenge of our Time, Oneworld Publications, Oxford, 1992

Tzu, Sun, *The Art of War*, Translated by Samuel B. Griffith, Oxford University Press, London, 1963

US Dept. of the Treasury: Treasury International Capital Data, Washington, D.C., various years

Vernon, R., *The Location of Economic Activity*, in: Dunning, J. (Ed.)Economic Analysis and Multinational Enterprise, London, England, 1974

Walter, Ingo and Areskoug, Kaj, *International Economics*, Third Edition, John Wiley and Sons, New York, 1981

Wikipedia, *Mercantilism,* Cyberspace
---, Foreign Direct Investment, Cyberspace